Report

TWELFTH

Annual ✦ Report

OF THE

Board of Trustees

OF THE

PUBLIC LIBRARY

OF THE

CITY OF MILWAUKEE,

OCTOBER 1, 1889.

STANDARD PRINTING CO., 114 MICHIGAN ST.,
MILWAUKEE.

TWELFTH

ANNUAL REPORT

OF THE

BOARD OF TRUSTEES

OF THE

P.UBLIC LIBRARY

OF THE

CITY OF MILWAUKEE.

OCTOBER 1ST, 1889.

MILWAUKEE.
STANDARD PRINTING COMPANY.
1889.

LIBRARY SERVICE.

KLAS AUGUST LINDERFELT, Librarian and Secretary.

CATALOGUING AND REFERENCE DEPARTMENTS.
THERESA HUBBELL WEST, Sup't and Deputy Librarian.
WILLY SCHMIDT, Assistant.

ISSUING DEPARTMENT.
MINNIE MYRTLE OAKLEY, Superintendent.
HARRIET ISABELLE WHITE, Assistant.
BELLE BLEND, Assistant.
KARIN SCHUMACHER, Assistant.
LOUIS SEVILLE RANDALL, Assistant.
WILLIAM PLATT POWELL, Evening Assistant.

READING ROOMS.
EVA SHEAFE COE, Superintendent.
AGNES SULLIVAN, Assistant.

JANITOR.
HEINRICH SCHWARTZ.

NIGHT WATCHMAN.
DAVID EDWARD DALE.

REPORT OF THE BOARD OF TRUSTEES

To the Common Council of the City of Milwaukee:

GENTLEMEN:

In accordance with the provisions of the law for the establishment of a public library in the city of Milwaukee, the Board of Trustees herewith submits its twelfth annual report, including a detailed report by the librarian on the work and records of the library for the past year.

The state legislature, at its last session, authorized your honorable body to issue bonds of the city of Milwaukee to the amount of $60,000, in order to procure means for the purchase of a suitable site for the erection of a building to accommodate both the public library and the public museum. The Board of Trustees, therefore, takes this opportunity to state a few of the considerations which, in their opinion, should govern the selection of a site for this purpose.

In the first place, it is absolutely necessary, for the best interests of the community, that a building destined to be occupied by two such important institutions as the library and the museum, both of which are daily visited by hundreds of persons, the combined number of visitors frequently exceeding one thousand in a single day, should be centrally located, that is but slightly, if at all, removed from the actual focus of the city's life, whether that be the geographical center or not. One of the largest cities of the eastern states affords us a practical object-lesson in the possession of a magnificent library building, costing upwards of a million of dollars, but used considerably less than the average New England village library, for the simple reason that it has been placed more than a mile and a half from the point where the business and life of the city centers.

Another question of great importance is the provision, at the start, of enough room for subsequent additions. Experience, even in this respect, has been dearly bought by other communities, and it behooves us to profit by what they have learned. The city of Boston has nearly finished her *third* new building for the public library in a new locality, a removal in each case being necessitated by the circumstance that all the available space for additions was exhausted. A library that has reached a certain size increases at a tremendous rate, since all the private collections of any size and value, within the radius of its influence, naturally gravitate toward it by means of bequest and otherwise. The fact that the library of which we have charge has grown in eleven years, from a very small beginning and with comparatively small resources, to the respectable size of 50,000 volumes, shows what its growth in the future is likely to be. As to a natural history museum of the extent and importance of the one belonging to the city, everybody knows what an amount of space is required for the proper and profitable exhibition of its collections.

The Board of Trustees therefore ventures to express the hope that the selection by the respective Boards of the Library and the Museum, of a site, for the new building will be made exclusively with the object in view of providing ample grounds for all time to come in a central location.

For the Board of Trustees of the Milwaukee Public Library,

MATTHEW KEENAN,
President.

ANNUAL REPORT OF LIBRARIAN.

MILWAUKEE, October 1st, 1889.

To the board of trustees of the Milwaukee public library.

GENTLEMEN: In accordance with your rules for the government of this library, I have the honor to submit herewith my report as librarian and secretary, on the condition and work of the library for the official year ending August 31, 1889, being the twelfth annual report since the organization of the library.

While the year just passed differs in nothing from the preceding ones, as far as the work and growth of the library is concerned, it is gratifying to report that, in response to the earnest words of your president in the last annual report, a beginning has been made toward securing for the library a permanent home in a not too far distant future. At the session of the Wisconsin State legislature, held during last winter, a bill was passed and became a law, authorizing the Common Council of the City of Milwaukee to issue bonds to the amount of $60,000, for the purpose of buying a suitable site, with a view of ultimately erecting thereon a building for the public library and the public museum. Steps are now being taken by the Common Council to carry out the provisions of this act, and it is therefore reasonable to hope that substantial progress will soon be made toward a satisfactory settlement of this matter, which is of so vital importance for both of these educational institutions.

The statistics of library work for the year, following the same arrangement as that employed in previous reports, are as follows:

BOOKS.

The number of bound volumes in the library at the close of last report was 46,357. During the year 2,444 volumes were added, of which number 1,642 volumes were acquired by purchase, 436 volumes consisted of magazines and pamphlets bound and placed permanently on the shelves, and the remaining 366 volumes were given to the library by various persons and institutions, a detailed statement of which will be found in appendix E. During the same time, 136 volumes were worn out and discarded as unserviceable, and 10 volumes were lost and paid for by borrowers. The book account, therefore, at the end of the year stands as follows:

On hand Sept. 1, 1888..46,357 vols.

Added up to Aug. 31, 1889:

By gift as per appendix E.................................... 366 vols.
By purchase and exchange................................1,642 "
By transfer by binding.. 436 "
　　　　　　　　　　　　　　　　　　　　　　———— 2,444 vols.

Total..48,801 vols.
Deduct books discarded................................ ...... 136 vols.
　　" 　　" 　　lost and paid for......................... . 　10 "
　　　　　　　　　　　　　　　　　　　　　　———— 146 vols.

In the library at the close of the year....................................48,665 vols.

The number of unbound pamphlets received during the year, that have not been bound up at once in book form, is 587, of which 3 were acquired by purchase, while 584 were given to the library, as per detailed statement in appendix E.

CLASSIFICATION OF ACCESSIONS.

The new books added to the library during the year belong to the following classes :

	Volumes.	Percentage.
General and bibliographical works	358	14.7
Philosophy and ethics	35	1.4
Religion and theology	140	5.7
Social and political science	341	14.
Philology	28	1.1
Natural science	159	6.5
Useful arts	119	4.9
Fine arts	101	4.1
Literature in general	159	6.5
Poetry and drama	89	3.6
Prose fiction and children's books	539	22.1
History	160	6.5
Geography and travels	77	3.2
Biography	139	5.7
	2444	100.

Of the whole number of books added, 2,263 volumes were in the English, 134 in the German, 39 in the French, and 8 in other languages.

COST OF BOOKS.

The amount expended for books and pamphlets during the year is $2,390.19, which, however, includes $174.12 paid on account of books received during the year embraced in last report. Deducting this amount and adding $156.23, which was audited and paid, after the close of this report, for books counted among the accessions of the year, shows that the actual cost of the books added to the library was $2,372.30.

It being found necessary to so regulate the finances of the library, without reference to the official library year, as to agree with the financial year of the general city government, which coincides with the calendar year, a larger balance for the second half of this year has been provided than heretofore, and, in consequence, a smaller amount of money has been expended for books, and fewer volumes purchased than for some time in the past. With the next calendar year, however, there will be a corresponingly increased amount available for the purchase of books.

BINDING.

The number of volumes rebound during the year is 350, while 78 volumes were resewed and put back in the old covers. During the same period, 154 new books and pamphlets, 417 magazines and 6 newspapers were bound. In addition to this, 115 volumes of newspapers, constituting the files of the Sentinel, News and other Milwaukee daily and weekly publications, were rebound, repaired, and put in good condition for future preservation. The total amount paid for all of this work is $978.72. Minor repairs on books, as well as labeling and fitting the new books for circulation, have been done by the regular library force, and the time of one attendant has been pretty well taken up with work of this nature.

CIRCULATION OF BOOKS.

In appendix A, will be found the usual detailed statement of the aggregate circulation of the library by months, and in appendix B, the record of the several delivery stations. This shows that the total number of books taken out for home use during 301 working days was 119,045, being a daily average of 376.8 volumes. The date of largest circulation was March 2, when 740 volumes were issued; and of the smallest, 191 volumes, June 26. The month of highest daily average of issue, 535, was April; and of the lowest, 291, September.

For comparison, I subjoin a statement of the circulation, by months, for the last three years:

MONTHS.	1886–7.		1887–8.		1888–9.	
	Working days.	Volumes issued.	Working days.	Volumes issued.	Working days.	Volumes issued.
September.....	25	5592	24½	6797	24	6839
October.........	26	6587	25½	8018	27	8048
November......	24	7494	25	8118	24	8923
December.......	26	7566	25	8425	24	9656
January.........	25	8687	25	9480	26	11341
February.......	23	10089	24	9947	23	11036
March..........	27	11327	27	11160	26	12589
April..............	25	9716	25	9347	25	13378
May..............	25	7488	26	9684	26	9749
June...............	26	7334	26	7702	25	11387
July..............	25	6866	25	7185	26	8520
August..........	27	7357	23	6891	24	7579
Total.............	304	97103	301	102754	300	119045
Daily average	319.4		341.3		376.8	

The circulation of books for home use shows a gratifying increase over that of last year, although that was larger than before. A part of this increase, particularly the very unusual number of books distributed in June, which otherwise generally is a month of comparatively small circulation, is attributable to the system of giving out books through the public schools, of which I shall speak further on. Through the delivery stations were sent out 13,842 volumes, and through the schools 6,728 volumes, while the branch library at Bay View circulated 3,463 volumes from the books permanently placed there. The number of books given out at the main library is, therefore, 95,012 volumes, an increase of nearly 7,000 volumes over last year, and these figures are irrespective of the use made of the reference and other books at the library rooms.

CLASSIFICATION OF CIRCULATION.

The percentage of circulation in the different classes of literature, for the last four years, is as follows:

	1885–6.	1886–7.	1887–8.	1888–9.
General works		1.4	4.1	4.2
Philosophy	.5	.8	.7	.7
Theology	.1	.1	1.1	.9
Social and political science	1.3	1.2	1.3	1.5
Philology	.1	.1	.2	.1
Natural science	1.6	2.	1.7	1.9
Useful arts	1.1	1.7	1.6	1.8
Fine arts	1.	1.6	1.7	1.5
Literature in general	7.	6.4	5.7	5.3
Prose fiction	62.	59.	58.2	56.9
Children's literature	13.	15.	14.4	14.7
History	4.2	4.	3.6	4.2
Geography and travels	4.	3.4	3.5	3.9
Biography	3.2	2.4	2.2	2.4

The most remarkable thing about this exhibit is the surprising stability of the relative percentage of the different classes of books circulated from year to year, no matter how the total number of books may vary. It must be remembered that the figures of the last column represent nearly 43,000 books more than those of the first, and these books selected from a stock larger by 14,000 volumes, and yet there is hardly any variation to speak of in the relative percentages of reading in the two years. To those, however, who believe that the reading of imaginative literature, particularly in the domain of prose fiction, is not beneficial, it must be gratifying to observe that the percentage of circulation of this class of books is slowly, but constantly, decreasing.

SCHOOL DISTRIBUTION.

Early in the present year, Mr. Anderson, the superintendent of schools of Milwaukee, and a member of your board, submitted a report on the circulation of the library, especially as regards the outlying districts of the city, and urged the necessity of instituting some scheme of making the library better known and appreciated among the children attending the public schools, which would indirectly result in bringing it home to their parents as well. After mature consideration, it was decided to give the teachers in the upper classes of certain schools the privilege of selecting from the library as many books as they could use to advantage for supplementary reading in their classes, to keep these books for six weeks, and during that time to have full control of them, so as to give them out to, and receive them back from the children as they saw fit. The library agreed to pay for the transportation of the books to and from the schools, and only required that the books should be given out to no one who was not provided with a library card in the usual way, so as to relieve the teacher from all responsibility for the book, while in the hands of a borrower, and that a report should be furnished with each book, when returned to the library, showing how many times it had been given out. A card was furnished with each book by the library, for the purpose of keeping this record. This experiment was put in operation during the latter part of February and continued until near the close of the schools in June. It proved an unqualified success in every way, and most of the teachers, who tried it, speak enthusiastically of its influence for good on the children under their charge. One teacher in a school situated in the northern extremity of the city, about four miles from the main library, says that hardly anyone in her district knew of the existence of the library and speaks graphically of the indignation of her scholars, when it was decided to call the books back to the library during the Easter vacation. Many of the children had drawn books on purpose to spend this vacation in reading them, and the teacher was obliged to promise to meet some of them at the library on the day after the books had been sent back, to help them get what they wanted from the library, without intervention of the school.

Under the arrangement agreed to, 2,235 books were drawn from the library by various teachers and given out 6,728 times, each volume thus being read on an average three times during the six weeks. The detailed statistics of the classes of books represented, and their respective circulation, will be found in appendix B.

The only difficulty attending this system of distribution, as far as observed, was that the library shelves were depleted of the more popular books, and it was very difficult for a child to get the books he wanted at the main library. To obviate this, it was decided at the last meeting of the library board for the year to spend an amount of $500 in duplicating the best books for young people, now in the library, and when these duplicates are received, one copy of the most called for will be reserved for the regular library circulation. With this restriction, the same policy of school distribution of books for supplementary reading will be pursued during the school year, just begun.

BOOK BORROWERS AND REGISTRATION.

The number of new registrations during the year was 4,781, making the total number of names registered up to the close of this report 35,840. Of this number, 27,261 cards have been called in from time to time, after running for two years, and canceled, as provided for in the regulations, leaving 8,579 cards now nominally in force. For various other causes, such as removal from the city, failure to pay fines, withdrawal of guaranty, etc., 297 cards were canceled during the year. Of the new cards, twenty-seven were issued in consideration of the stipulated money deposit, and twenty-three such deposits were withdrawn, leaving thirteen deposits still on hand.

READING ROOM.

The total number of visitors to the reading room during the 300 week days it was open, was 58,704, being a daily average of 196. On application, 4,991 magazines were delivered from the counter, or an average of 17 per day, all the rest of the periodicals being kept on the tables, open to all comers, without any kind of registration. On 52 Sunday afternoons, the number of visitors was 6,816, an average attendance of 131, and 854 magazines, or 16 each day, were drawn for reading.

For the same reason mentioned above, in speaking of the purchase of books, quite a number of periodicals, comprising 13 daily newspapers in the English, and 7 in other languages, 18 weekly publications in English, and 4 in other languages, and 8 English monthlies, were dropped from the subscription list of the library in the early part of the new year. There are now kept on file 210 serial publications, of which 136 are magazines of general interest or for special purposes, and 74 newspapers. The number of magazines is made up of 80 American, 36 English, 4 French and 16 German publications. The newspapers comprise 27 dailies, 47 weeklies, semi-monthlies and monthlies, representing the United States, Canada, England, Scotland, Ireland, and Germany. Forty-two news-papers and three magazines are furnished to the library free of charge, a detailed statement of which will be found in appendix E. The total amount expended on this department during the year is $1,026.03. Copies of the monthly numbers of Harper's Magazine, Century Magazine, Scribner's Magazine, Atlantic Monthly, Lippincott's Magazine, St. Nicholas, Wide Awake, and Harper's Young People have been furnished for home use, as during the preceding year.

REFERENCE ROOM.

This room has been very much used during the last year, particularly by students in the various schools and colleges of the city, and the only regret is that it is not possible, with the present accommodations of the library, to furnish them with more room and better facilities for reading and study. As before, no attempt has been made to collect statistics of the use of books in this room, nor of the number of persons availing themselves of its privileges, except during the 52 Sunday afternoons, when there were in all 1,560 readers during the year, being an average of 30 each Sunday, the highest number being 41, in November, and the smallest, 18, in July.

PORTRAIT COLLECTION.

The collection of portraits in the Reading room has received the following additions as gifts during the year: From Julius Goldschmidt, an excellent crayon portrait of Peter Engelmann, a well-known teacher of this city and founder of the German-English Academy; from Bernard Goldsmith, a portrait of his brother, Captain Gustavus Goldsmith, who fell at the battle of Chickamauga from Mrs. Alex. Mitchell, a fine crayon portrait of her self, as a pendant to the portrait of her husband, received before; and from Daniel Wells, junior, a portrait in crayon of himself.

CATALOGUING.

The cataloguing of new accessions has been done by the same force as before. Four new numbers of the Quarterly Index of Additions have been published during the year, ending with No. 12. The cost of printing these, including the last number issued during the previous year, together with the author and title-index to volume 1, is $687.30.

At the request of the Superintendent of Schools, a preliminary catalogue of books in the library, suitable for young people, including 1600 titles, has been prepared, and will be printed as a supplement to a Teachers' Manual, issued by the School Board. Copies of this catalogue will be struck off for use in the library, and will serve as the groundwork for the fuller, detailed catalogue, with age classification and notes, which is contemplated under the instructions received from your board.

Of the general catalogue of 1885, 10 copies were sold during the year for $27.40, and two copies were given out on deposit. The amount received for copies sold of the Quarterly Index of Additions is $8.95.

ADMINISTRATION.

The library force remains the same, as to number and distribution of work, as at the end of last year, and the aggregate amount paid out for salaries of all kinds, not including those of the keepers of the stations, is $7,981.67.

The cost of maintaining the delivery stations, including the salaries paid to the keepers, and the amount paid the Lightning Messenger and Express Co. for cartage during the year, is $901.75.

INSURANCE.

After a thorough examination of the value of the library property, and taking into consideration the great danger from fire in its present location, it was decided to increase the insurance on the library with $15,000. The whole amount of insurance carried is therefore $65,000, distributed among the following companies:

Ætna Insurance Co., Hartford	$2,500
Allemannia Fire Insurance Co., Pittsburg	2,500
Amazon Insurance Co., Cincinnati	2,500
Boatman's Fire and Marine Insurance Co., Pittsburg	2,500
British America Assurance Co., Toronto	2,500
Buffalo German Insurance Co.	2,500
Citizens' Insurance Co., Pittsburg	2,500
Concordia Fire Insurance Co., Milwaukee	5,000
Fire Insurance Co. of the County of Philadelphia	2,500
German Fire Insurance Co. of Peoria, Ill.	2,500
Glens Falls Insurance Co., Glens Falls, N. Y.	2,500
Insurance Company of North America, Philadelphia	2,500
Michigan Fire and Marine Insurance Co., Detroit	2,500
Milwaukee Mechanics' Insurance Co.	5,000
Norwich Union Fire Insurance Society, U. S. Branch, New York	2,500
Pennsylvania Fire Insurance Co., Philadelphia	2,500
Queen Insurance Co. of Liverpool, Western Dept., Chicago	2,500
Rhode Island Underwriters' Association, Providence	2,500
Rochester German Insurance Co.	2,500
Saint Paul Fire and Marine Insurance Co.	2,500
Security Insurance Co., New Haven	2,500
Sun Fire Office of London, U. S. Branch, Watertown, N. Y.	2,500
Western Assurance Co., Toronto	2,500
Williamsburg City Fire Insurance Co.	2,500

FINANCIAL REPORT.

In conclusion, I beg leave to submit the usual statement of the receipts and expenditures of the library during the year, including both the miscellaneous receipts of the librarian and the account with the city treasurer, as follows:

CASH ACCOUNT.

RECEIPTS.

Cash on hand September 1, 1888	$148.12
Fines for undue detention of books	357.94
Catalogues sold	27.40
Bulletins sold	8.95
Catalogue deposits	6.00
Security deposits	81.00
Books lost or damaged	11.34
Lost cards replaced	14.90
Miscellaneous	7.93

DISBURSEMENTS.

Security deposits refunded	$69.00
Refunded for lost books restored	2.92
Fines refunded	10
Paid city treasurer	533.30
Cash on hand August 31, 1889	58.26
	$663.58 $663.58

LIBRARY FUND ACCOUNT.

DEBIT.

Balance, as per last report....................................$3,339.78*)	
Paid by the librarian... 533.30	
Appropriation for 1888.......................................24,137.12	
— ——	$28,010.20

CREDIT.

Amount drawn on vouchers issued by your board
  during the official year on account of

Rent..$1,750.00	
Salaries... 7,981.67	
Fuel and gas.. 1,400.60	
Books.. 2,390.19	
Newspapers and periodicals................................. 1,026.03	
Postage, express and freight................................ 101.88	
Furniture and repairs.. 687.12	
Stationery and printing....................................... 471.90	
Printing quarterly additions............................... 687.30	
Insurance.. 577.50	
Binding... 978.72	
Delivery stations.. 901.75	
Miscellaneous... 261.48	
————	$19,216.14

Balance in library fund Sept. 1, 1889..........................$ 8,794.06

All of which is respectfully submitted.

K. A: LINDERFELT,

Librarian and Secretary.

---

*)$3,897.78, given in last report as the balance, was a misprint, as will appear
from the rest of the figures given.

APPENDIX A.
AGGREGATE CIRCULATION.

	Days open.	General works.	Philosophy.	Theology.	Social and political science.	Philology.	Natural science.	Useful arts.	Fine arts.	Literature.	Prose fiction.	Children's fiction.	History.	Geography.	Biography.	Total circulation.	Date and highest circulation.	Date and lowest circulation.	Daily average.	Number of cards issued.
September, 1838	24	284	50	6f	118	9	89	110	107	344	4,291	800	284	198	144	6,889	22—464	17—314	291	219
October, "	27	301	63	79	159	18	130	122	165	503	4,815	840	428	246	143	8,048	27—483	4—224	298	276
November, "	24	384	62	91	151	12	116	170	141	521	5,162	1,165	418	312	218	8,928	10—519	5—233	372	887
December, "	24	439	60	84	163	10	139	180	150	562	5,609	1,347	410	341	162	9,656	8—520	13—291	402	859
January, 1839	26	521	99	116	139	26	171	266	191	622	6,540	1,633	501	418	258	11,341	26—677	8—223	486	548
February, "	28	482	88	112	147	22	188	202	188	597	6,543	1,292	497	424	260	11,086	2—710	5—375	480	1120
March, "	26	591	92	144	183	14	266	275	245	778	7,152	1,488	555	508	348	12,559	2—740	28—346	484	729
April, "	25	585	65	124	151	7	416	265	199	728	6,894	2,527	648	800	479	13,378	13—655	23—312	535	504
May, "	26	426	60	91	159	4	161	183	164	453	5,689	1,588	286	304	282	9,749	25—564	17—283	375	268
June, "	25	404	70	86	136	6	344	232	108	554	5,897	2451	654	687	348	11,887	1—647	23—191	455	199
July, "	26	341	66	58	114	14	137	120	162	348	5,297	1,868	202	231	127	8,520	29—484	13—280	328	176
August, "	24	276	53	52	118	13	106	118	92	319	4,825	1,151	189	178	94	7,579	31—488	23—224	316	165
TOTAL	300	4,984	828	1,098	1,788	150	2,258	2,182	1,852	6,819	67,713	17,561	4,962	4,592	2,808	119,045	740	191	376.8	4,781
PER CENT		4.2	.7	.9	1.5	.1	1.9	1.8	1.5	5.8	56.9	14.7	4.2	3.9	2.4					

APPENDIX B.
CIRCULATION OF DELIVERY STATIONS.
A.—SOUTH SIDE.

	Days open	General works	Philosophy	Theology	Social and political science	Philology	Natural science	Useful arts	Fine Arts	Literature	Prose fiction	Children's fiction	History	Geography	Biography	Total circulation	Date and highest circulation	Date and lowest circulation	Daily average
September, 1888	25	5	1		2			2	1	1	120	41	6	5	4	188	7—17	1—2	8
October, "	27	1		1	2			7		1	123	55	4	1	2	200	27—13	20—3	8
November, "	24			1	2			3	3	4	122	39	3	8	1	183	8—21	19—3	7
December, "	24	1					2	5	1	2	151	65	7	2	2	237	27—24	10—3	10
January, 1889	26	6	1		1		1	6		8	139	63	8	5	1	240	14—18	28—3	9
February, "	23	2	1		3		6	6		5	176	76	5	13	5	298	26—27	11—3	12
March, "	26	1			4	1	6	9		9	234	82	11	17		386	30—25	11—5	15
April, "	25	4			2	2	6	3		11	186	82	13	17	1	319	27—21	1—4	13
May, "	26		1		2	1	1	3		7	165	104	9	11	1	297	3—33	1—6	12
June, "	25	2	2	2	2		6	6		4	138	122	4	4	1	290	22—20	24—3	11
July, "	26	1			2		4	6	1	4	119	94	5	9	7	252	22—15	29—2	10
August, "	24			1	2		1	7		8	131	68	5	6	1	230	31—19	2—4	10
TOTAL	301	28	5	5	24	1	33	59	7	64	1804	891	83	91	25	3120	33		210.4
PER CENT.		.9	.2	.2	.8	.1	1.1	1.9	.2	2.	57.8	28.5	2.7	2.9	.8				

APPENDIX B.

CIRCULATION OF DELIVERY STATIONS.—(Continued.)

B.—EAST SIDE.

	Days open	General works	Philosophy	Theology	Social and political science	Philology	Natural science	Useful arts	Fine arts	Literature	Prose fiction	Children's fiction	History	Geography	Biography	Total circulation	Date and highest circulation	Date and lowest circulation	Daily average
September, 1888	25	2	2	4	5	1	3	5	22	31	236	45	5	12	7	379	20—25	10—6	15
October, "	27	6	2	9	7	1	6	9	5	25	218	61	7	3	8	370	6—30	31—6	14
November, "	24	4	5	11	4	1	2	6	6	13	177	51	8	3	2	293	8—25	23—7	12
December, "	24	6	5	2	8		1	9	6	12	149	57	5	8	5	268	3—18	17—4	11
January, 1889	26	8	1	7	5	1		10	5	7	177	41	6	6	3	279	19—20	10—2	11
February, "	23	12	1	2	3		2	5	3	2	174	39	12	2	5	268	16—18	11—5	12
March, "	26	17	2	3	4	1	5	6	6	21	187	46	18	5		312	21—20	18—4	12
April, "	25	12	3	1	4	1	5	7	2	24	181	33	8	11	8	296	24—27	29—5	12
May, "	26	4	3		5	1	8	12	6	11	203	65	5	8	8	332	3—22	27—3	13
June, "	25	2			2		3	18	5	7	195	70	4	3	6	326	27—22	24—7	13
July, "	26	6	3		8	4	5	7	3	5	179	51	3	5	3	274	19—17	12—5	10
August, "	24	4		4			5	9	3	11	173	34	3	9	1	264	13—22	30—4	11
TOTAL	301	83	23	46	59	9	40	103	70	174	2249	593	84	75	48	3661	30		212.2
PER CENT		2.3	.8	1.3	1.6	.2	1.1	2.8	1.9	4.8	61.4	16.2	2.3	.2	1.3				

APPENDIX B.

CIRCULATION OF DELIVERY STATIONS.—(Continued.)

C.—THIRD STREET.

	Days open.	General works.	Philosophy.	Theology.	Social and political science.	Philology.	Natural science.	Useful arts.	Fine arts.	Literature.	Prose fiction.	Children's fiction.	History.	Geography.	Biography.	Total circulation.	Date and highest circulation.	Date and lowest circulation.	Daily average.
September, 1888	25	8	3	3		2	4	7	6	10	109	15	3	3	4	177	28—12	10—3	7
October, "	27	8		2	5	1	3	5	2	8	119	15	18	11		197	31—16	29—2	7
November, "	24	6		2	6	1		6	3	11	115	20	10	15		195	16—14	26—2	8
December, "	24	9	4			2	2	3		9	116	42	11	7	2	201	1—17	29—3	8
January, 1889	26	8	1	2	1	2	3	4	4	7	117	41	14	12		217	11—17	4—2	9
February, "	23	14	6	1			3	4	13	9	110	42	7	4		209	27—16	4—3	9
March, "	26	13	1	4	4		7	5	5	7	118	41	15	8		229	21—20	25—1	9
April, "	25	13					5	9	6	4	121	57	17	7		246	17—15	19—3	10
May, "	26	13		3	5		8	9	5	9	108	57	10	7		234	3—20	11—2	9
June, "	25	11	1	2	8		5	10	4	9	97	70	4		4	221	12—20	10—3	9
July, "	26	6	2	1	1		1	5	4	3	82	69	3	1	4	184	22—11	15—2	7
August, "	24	2		1		1	6	5	1	3	57	34	3			117	9—10	16—1	9
TOTAL	301	111	18	21	30	9	47	73	53	89	1269	503	115	75	14	2427	20	1	8.1
PER CENT		4.6	.7	.8	1.2	.4	1.9	3.	2.2	3.7	52.3	20.7	4.8	3.1	.6				

APPENDIX B—(Continued.)

CIRCULATION OF BAY VIEW BRANCH LIBRARY.

	Days open.	General works.	Philosophy.	Theology.	Social and political science.	Philology.	Natural science.	Useful arts.	Fine arts.	Literature.	Prose fiction.	Children's fiction.	History.	Geography.	Biography.	Total circulation.	Date and highest circulation.	Date and lowest circulation.	Daily average.
September, 1888	25								1	10	113	9	9	11	11	162	7—13	5—2	6
October, "	27									13	138	20	8	10	8	199	23—12	17—2	7
November, "	24	1								17	192	16	6	10	18	260	24—21	2—3	11
December, "	24			1						18	168	26	8	12	18	254	26—16	21—3	11
January, 1889	26	1		1			1			19	208	57	5	19	14	330	26—22	4—4	8
February, "	23	4		3	4		3	3		25	242	56	11	19	15	372	23—29	28—8	16
March, "	26		1	2	2		1			23	250	57	7	13	16	368	13—24	10—6	14
April, "	25		1	1	1			1		24	222	43	9	9	18	337	2—27	28—7	13
May, "	25		3	1						23	214	23	9	16	18	310	13—24	22—8	12
June, "	26		1					1		14	232	23	5	12	8	306	1—23	22—4	12
July, "	26	1	1							13	215	36	5	11	12	296	20—23	31—4	11
August, "	24		1					1		13	210	24	7	7	9	269	26—22	15—6	11
TOTAL	301	12	10	8	7		7	7		206	2400	423	86	137	162	3463		29	11.5
PER CENT		.3	.3	.2	.2		.2	.2		6.	69.3	12.2	2.5	4.	4.7				11.5

CIRCULATION OF DELIVERY STATIONS.—(Continued.)

F.—GRAND OPERA HOUSE.

	Days open.	General works.	Philosophy.	Theology.	Social and political science.	Philology.	Natural science.	Useful arts.	Fine arts.	Literature.	Prose fiction.	Children's fiction.	History.	Geography.	Biography.	Total circulation.	Date and highest circulation.	Date and lowest circulation.	Daily average.
September, 1888.	25				16				1	8	33	3	2	1		64	18—5	25—1	3
October, "	27		6		21				2	6	27	1	16		1	73	8—5	20—1	3
November, "	24		3		27		1	1	3	31	25		15	1		78	15—5	21—2	3
December, "	24		7	2	22			1	1	15	15		8			63	28—4	29—1	2
January, 1889.	26		6		17			3	2	19	11	5	6	3	2	83	31—6	25—2	3
February, "	23		3		11			5	3	16	28	1	9	1	1	87	5—1	5—1	3
March, "	26		1		13		3	9	1	15	40	1	14	20		101	25—6	12—2	4
April, "	25		1		13		1	5	2	16	37	6	6	5	1	109	26—6	8—3	4
May, "	26		3		23			3	3	9	38	11	5	8		102	25—7	23—2	4
June, "	25		4		28		1	2	1	14	41	2	3	9	1	102	6—7	24—3	4
July, "	26		4		20		3			10	53	8	10	7	1	113	1—5	6—3	4
August, "	24		5		13		6		2	4	46	4		4		94	30—8	13—1	4
Total	301		30	4	224		16	30	14	155	394	37	90	67	8	1069	8	1	
Per Cent.			2.8	.4	20.9		1.5	2.8	1.3	14.5	37.	3.4	8.4	6.3	.7				3.6

APPENDIX B.

CIRCULATION OF DELIVERY STATIONS.—(Continued.)

E.—BAY VIEW.

	Days open.	General works.	Philosophy.	Theology.	Social and political science.	Philology.	Natural science.	Useful arts.	Fine arts.	Literature.	Prose fiction.	Children's fiction.	History.	Geography.	Biography.	Total circulation.	Date and highest circulation.	Date and lowest circulation.	Daily average.
September, 1888	25							1	2	3	40	9	2	2	1	57	26—5	10—1	2
October, "	27								3	4	34	3	1	6		55	31—4	27—1	2
November, "	24			1			3	1		3	44	7	1	3		65	21—8	1—1	3
December, "	24	1		1	1		3	2		2	47	8	1	5		70	21—5	3—1	3
January, 1889	26			1			1	4	2	2	53	10	1	1	2	75	23—7	22—1	3
February, "	23						2	1	2	1	59	11				79	26—7	7—1	3
March, "	26				1		2	1	2	3	71	4		1		91	4—5	26—1	3
April, "	25						1	3	4	3	64	13	8	7	3	97	16—9	25—1	4
May, "	26						2	1	1	5	67	29	7	4	2	111	4—5	31—2	4
June, "	25							1	3	3	64	19		8		101	19—6	20—2	4
July, "	26	4						1	1	3	52	4		6	2	69	2—6	27—1	2
August, "	24	2						1		1	60	4		2	2	75	31—7	26—1	3
TOTAL	301	7		3	2		14	15	17	33	655	121	22	44	12	945	9	1	
PER CENT.		.7		.3	.2		1.5	1.6	1.8	3.5	69.3	12.8	2.3	4.7	1.3				3.1

CIRCULATION OF DELIVERY STATIONS.—(Continued.)

D.—WALNUT STREET.

	Days open.	General works.	Philosophy.	Theology.	Social and political science.	Philology.	Natural science.	Useful arts.	Fine Arts.	Literature.	Prose fiction.	Children's fiction.	History.	Geography.	Biography.	Total circulation.	Date and highest circulation.	Date and lowest circulation.	Daily average.
September, 1888	25	1		1	1		2	1	1	4	78	23	2	4		121	22–10	3–2	5
October, "	27	1					4	9		11	132	31	4	2		192	31–29	1–1	7
November, "	24			6			4			14	122	22	4	6		179	8–23	26–2	7
December, "	24	6	1	6	8		6		5	12	149	57	5	8	5	268	3–18	17–4	11
January, 1889	26			2			9	2	1	8	123	38	6	12	1	196	3–15	2–3	7
February, "	23			1			6		2	7	161	59	17	4		261	28–23	16–3	10
March, "	26	1	1	1	1		9	3	3	11	165	57	13	13		268	30–17	4–3	11
April, "	26	3	1	2	1		9	2	2	12	169	58	11	7	3	280	16–25	9–5	10
May, "	25			1	1		5	7	3	1	121	74	5	13		225	3–26	17–4	9
June, "	26		1	1	1		9	2	2	6	127	76	6	8	3	226	11–22	27–3	7
July, "	25		1	1			3	2	3	6	127	71	2	3		189	15–15	18–3	9
August, "	24			1			3	4	3	7	126	59	4	7	1	215	31–24	5–2	9
TOTAL	301	13	3	17	12		51	32	21	94	1572	625	79	80	21	2620			
PER CENT.	.5	.1	.6	.5			1.9	1.2	.8	3.6	60.	23.9	3.	3.1	.8		29	1	8.7

APPENDIX B—(Continued).

CIRCULATION THROUGH SCHOOLS.—1888-9.

Month	General works	Philosophy	Theology	Social and political science	Philology	Natural science	Useful arts	Fine arts	Literature	Prose fiction	Children's fiction	History	Geography	Biography	Total
September, 1888															
October, "															
November, "															
December, "															
January, 1889															
February, "		4				4			4			6	1		20
March, "	13		10	12		85	29	20	50	33	156	42	92	96	637
April, "	78		5	9		259	72	17	149	159	1326	254	415	223	2971
May, "				2		12	2	5	4	23	244	23	31	53	404
June, "	48		24	3		218	69	19	128	149	1087	327	413	207	2696
July, "															
August, "															
TOTAL	139	4	48	26		578	172	61	335	364	2818	652	952	579	6728
PER CENT	2.1	.1	.7	.4		8.6	2.5	.9	5.	5.4	41.9	9.7	14.1	8.6	

APPENDIX C.

READING ROOM.

| | DAYS OPEN | | READERS | | | MAGAZINES. | | | DAILY AVERAGE. | | | |
| | | | | | | | | | READERS | | MAGAZINES | |
	Sec. days.	Sun-days.	Secular days.	Sun-days.	Total.	Secular days.	Sun-days.	Total.	Secul'r Days.	Sun-days.	Secul'r Days.	Sun-days.
September, 1888	24	5	4,502	687	5,189	277	46	323	192	137	12	9
October, "	27	4	5,695	556	6,251	412	59	471	211	139	15	15
November, "	24	4	3,746	478	4,224	529	73	602	156	119	22	18
December, "	24	5	4,031	629	4,660	464	177	641	168	126	19	35
January, 1889	26	4	4,961	411	5,372	452	52	504	191	103	17	13
February, "	23	4	5,042	627	5,669	567	57	624	219	157	25	14
March, "	26	5	6,669	985	7,654	508	97	605	257	197	19	19
April, "	25	4	6,822	912	7,734	376	79	455	273	228	15	20
May, "	26	4	6,053	490	6,543	360	51	411	233	122	14	13
June, "	25	5	4,222	543	4,765	344	74	418	169	109	14	15
July, "	26	4	3,595	259	3,854	413	48	461	138	65	16	12
August, "	24	4	3,366	239	3,605	289	41	330	180	59	12	10
TOTAL	300	52	58,704	6,816	65,520	4,991	854	5,845	196	131	17	16

COMPARATIVE SUMMARY OF STATISTICS.

	1878*	1878-9.	1879-80.	1880-1.	1881-2.	1882-3.
Books in Library, beginning of year	9,958	10,024	15,290	16,410	18,649	21,742
Total accessions	66	6,087	1,399	2,447	3,166	2,778
Given	65	149	159	162	833	505
Transferred by binding		88	87	161	146	217
Purchased	1	5,850	1,153	2,124	2,187	2,056
Cost of books actually received	$18 00	$3,834 90	$1,560 52	$3,329 97	$2,640 10	$3,671 53
Worn out and discarded	1	807	262	109	50	28
Lost, sold and exchanged	4	14	17	13	23	10
Pamphlets, accessions		43	168	326	366	516
Registered book borrowers, beg. of year		1,957	5,350	7,318	10,670	12,888
New names registered	1,957	3,193	1,968	3,351	2,218	2,672
Circulation of books	8,692	91,296	86,328	97,874	88,331	83,052
Working days	48	305½	273	306	305	289
Daily average	181.8	298.8	316.3	319.8	289.8	287.4
Largest issue in one day	327	647	610	697	601	773
Smallest issue in one day	.72	132	102	156	101	47
Number of books fined	193	4,680	3,649	4,201	3,439	4,357
Received for fines	$15 53	$394 24	$304 14	$378 13	$303 25	$341 51
Reading room—Magazines on file	28	31	33	70	75	84
Newspapers on file	67	69	64	97	107	107
Visitors				47,467	70,686	66,589
Days open				306	305	289
Average daily attendance				155	232	230
Magazines delivered				6,120	7,646	6,879
Sunday readers		915	4,168	7,141	8,100	8,098
Sundays open		19	48	51	52	50
Average attendance on Sundays		48	87	140	156	162
Magazines delivered				1,063	866	867
Cost of serials	$298 44	$609 12	$438 28	$773 50	$887 33	$887 65
Binding and repairing—Number volumes		1,693	1,823	1,000	1,793	892
Cost of binding and repairing		$560 83	$601 45	$443 63	$689 27	$366 63
Appropriation	$8,923 76	$9,330 00	$11,000 00	$11,300 00	$15,567 98	$17,996 87
Amount paid for salaries	$795 35	$3,428 35	$4,075 97	$5,032 28	$5,040 00	$5,351 16

*The statistics for this year comprise only seven weeks from July 8, 1878, when the library was opened to the public.

COMPARATIVE SUMMARY OF STATISTICS—(Continued).

	1883-4	1884-5	1885-6	1886-7	1887-8	1888-9
Books in Library at beginning of year	24,481	28,785	32,499	35,695	42,665	46,357
Total accessions	4,640	3,842	3,407	7,199	3,920	2,444
Given	393	759	450	492	557	366
Transferred by binding	306	207	22	474	240	436
Purchased	3,941	2,876	2,934	5,253	3,123	1,638
Cost of books actually received	$7,196 67	$5,266 72	$5,067 88	$7,931 48	$5,873 52	$2,372 30
Worn out and discarded	283	116	170	227	219	136
Lost, sold and exchanged	53	12	41	2	9	15
Pamphlets, accessions	339	458	256	647	523	587
Registered book borrowers, beg. of year	15,560	18,286	20,962	23,760	27,410	31,059
New names registered	2,726	2,676	2,795	3,650	3,649	4,781
Circulation of books	87,341	81,399	76,375	97,103	102,754	119,045
Working days	306	281	279	304	301	300
Daily average	285.4	289.7	273.7	319.4	341.3	376.8
Largest issue in one day	670	645	597	716	666	740
Smallest issue in one day	146	132	104	169	173	191
Number of books fined	4,760	4,427	3,794	3,812	3,998	4,867
Received for fines	$381 12	$278 80	$257 18	$234 82	$250 11	$357 94
Reading room—Magazines on file	95	98	102	115	144	136
Newspapers on file	113	119	117	119	116	74
Visitors	73,541	60,205	63,068	70,548	62,465	58,704
Days open	306	300	300	304	305	300
Average daily attendance	240	201	210	232	205	196
Magazines delivered	7,892	5,043	4,926	4,560	5,277	4,991
Sunday readers	8,620	7,719	8,504	8,435	8,152	6,816
Sundays open	53	51	50	52	49	52
Average attendance on Sundays	163	151	170	162	166	131
Magazines delivered	914	961	744	742	608	854
Cost of serials	$963 49	$1,099 00	$1,149 83	$1,228 96	$1,267 96	$1,026 03
Binding and repairing—number volumes	2,020	1,914	1,544	2,339	1,855	2,120
Cost of binding and repairing	$1,090 45	$967 29	$730 81	$989 89	$905 13	$978 72
Appropriation	$18,737 93	$19,715 34	$19,715 34	$20,660 44	$22,243 04	$24,137 12
Amount paid for salaries	$5,792 40	$6,151 21	$6,710 17	$7,097 60	$7,929 32	$7,981 67

APPENDIX E.

LIST OF GIFTS TO THE LIBRARY.

	Volumes.	Pamphlets.
Abbey, Mrs. M. O., Milwaukee	1	
Aberdeen, Scotland, public library		1
Albany, N. Y., young men's association		1
Allen, W. F., Madison, Wis.	1	
American bar association, Philadelphia	7	
American federation of labor, New York, N. Y.		1
Amherst, Mass., college		2
Appleton, D., & Co., New York	1	
Arnold, Mrs. S. D., Milwaukee	22	
Astor library, New York, N. Y.		27
Ayer Co., J. C., Lowell, Mass.	1	
Baltimore, Md., New mercantile library association....		1
Beloit, Wis., college		1
Birchard library, Fremont, O.		1
Birmingham, England, free libraries		1
Bissell, W. S., Buffalo, N. Y.	2	
Black, W. N.	1	
Boston, Mass., Athenæum (various bulletins).		
" " public library	1	5
Braun & Schneider, München, Germany	1	
Bridgeport, Conn., public library		4
Bronson library, Waterbury, Conn.		2
Brookline, Mass., public library		12
Brooklyn, N. Y., library		18
Brymner, D., Ottawa, Canada	1	
Buffalo, N. Y., library		27
Buck, J. S., Milwaukee	1	
Butler, J. D., Madison, Wis.	1	
California, state bureau of labor statistics	1	
" " mining bureau, Sacramento, Cal.		1
" university, Berkeley, Cal.		3

Wisconsin secretary of state	1	
" state board of health	1	
" state board of supervision	1	
" state historical society		2
" state library	1	
" state superintendent of public property	8	1
" " " of public schools		1
" university	1	1
*Worcester, Mass., free public library		1
Wright, A. G., Milwaukee	1	
Wright, Samuel, Milwaukee	23	
Yale university library, New Haven, Conn		4
	366	587

*Also various bulletins.

APPENDIX F.

NEWSPAPERS AND MAGAZINES ON FILE.

IN THE GENERAL READING ROOM.

AMERICA.

Atlanta, Ga., Southern industrial railroad record, M. (Gift of the publishers.)

Battle Creek, Mich., Herold der wahrheit, (*German*), SM. (Gift of the publishers.)

Boston, Mass., Christian register, W. (Gift of the publishers.)
    Civil service record, Irr. (Gift of the publishers.)
    Globe, D.
    Literary world, SM.
    Office, M.
    Our dumb animals, M. (Gift of the publishers.)
    Popular science news, M.
    Youth's companion, W.

Chicago, Ill., America, W.
    Dial, M.
    Gamla och nya hemlandet, (*Swedish*), W. (Gift of the publishers.)
    Illinois Staatszeitung, (*German*), D.
    Open court, W.
    Our young folks' monthly, M. (Gift of the publishers.)
    Skandinaven, (*Norwegian*), D.
    Times, D.
    Tribune, D.
    Union signal, W. (Gift of the publishers.)

Cleveland, O., Silver dollar, SM. (Gift of the publishers.)

Detroit, Mich., Der arme teufel, (*German*), W. (Gift of the publishers.)

Madison, Wis., Northwestern mail, W. (Gift of the publishers.)
    State journal, D.

Medford, Wis., Ansiedler in Wisconsin, (*German*), M.
　　　Waldbote, (*German*), W.
Milwaukee, Wis., Amerikanische turnzeitung, (*German*), W.
　　　Arbeiter-zeitung, (*German*), D.
　　　Columbia, (*German*), W.
　　　Currie's monthly, M.
　　　Erziehungs-blätter, (*German*), M.
　　　Evening Wisconsin, D.
　　　Freidenker, (*German*), W.
　　　Freie presse, (*German*), D.
　　　Germania, (*German*), W.
　　　Haus- und bauernfreund, (*German*), W.
　　　Herold, (*German*), D.
　　　Journal, D.
　　　Kinder-post, (*German*), W.
　　　Local, W.
　　　News, D.
　　　Peck's sun, W.
　　　Proceedings of the common council, BW.
　　　Proceedings of the school board, M.
　　　Review, D.
　　　Saturday star, W.
　　　Seebote, (*German*), D.
　　　Sentinel, D.
　　　Social circle, W.
　　　Sonntagsblatt, (*German*), W.
　　　Sunday telegraph, W.
　　　Telephon. (*German*), W.
　　　Times, W.
　　　United states miller, M.
　　　Volks-magazin, (*German*), W.
　　　Vorwärts, (*German*), W.
　　　Weekly world, W.
　　　Yenowine's Sunday news, W.
　　　Young churchman, W.
　　　Zgoda, (*Polish*), W.

New Orleans, La., Picayune, D.
New York, N. Y., Bellestristisches journal, (*German*), W.
　　　Co-operative index to periodicals, Q.

New York, N. Y., Courier des Etats-Unis, (*French*), W.
>Engineering and building record, W.
>Epoch, W.
>Frank Leslie's illustrated newspaper, W.
>Garden and forest, W.
>Harper's weekly, W.
>Iron age, W.
>Literary news, M.
>Nation, W.
>Puck, W.
>Staatszeitung, (*German*), D.
>Stockholder, W. (Gift of the publishers).
>Tribune, D.
>Truth seeker, W. (Gift of the publishers).
>Voice, W. (Gift of the publishers).
>Volkszeitung, (*German*), D. (Gift of the publishers).
>World, D.

Oakland, Cal., American sentinel, W. (Gift of the publishers).
Philadelphia, Pa., American, W.
Pittsburg, Pa., Commercial gazette, D. (Gift of the publishers).
San Francisco, Cal., Chronicle, D.
Toronto, Ont., Globe, D.
Washington, D. C., Congressional record, D. (Gift).
>Public opinion, W.

FRANCE.

Paris, L'illustration, W.

GERMANY.

Berlin, Norddeutsche allgemeine zeitung, SD.
Halle, Natur, W.
Leipzig, Gartenlaube, W.
>Illustrirte zeitung, W.
Stuttgart, Ueber land und meer, W.

GREAT BRITAIN AND IRELAND.

Dublin, United Ireland, W.
Glasgow, Herald, W.
London, Academy, W.
>Athenæum, W.
>British journal of photography, W.
>Engineering, W.

London, Graphic, W.
  Illustrated news, W.
  Punch, W.
  Saturday review, W.
  Times, W.

IN THE LADIES' READING ROOM.

(IN ADDITION TO THOSE IN THE GENERAL ROOM.)

Beatrice, Neb., Woman's tribune, W. (Gift of the publishers.)
Boston, Mass., Woman's journal, W.
Milwaukee, Wis., Evening Wisconsin, D.
  Sentinel, D.
New York, N. Y., Dress, M.
  Harper's bazar, W.
  Harper's weekly, W.

ON APPLICATION AT THE COUNTER IN THE READING ROOM.

AMERICA.

American antiquarian, Chicago, BM.
American anthropologist, Washington, Q.
American architect and building news, Boston, W.
American chemical journal, Baltimore, BM.
American journal of archæology, Baltimore, Q.
American journal of mathematics, Baltimore, Q.
American journal of philology, Baltimore, Q.
American journal of science, New Haven, M.
American meteorological journal, Detroit, M.
American microscopical journal, Washington, M. (Gift of the publishers.)
American naturalist, Philadelphia, M.
Andover review, Boston, M.
Architectural era, Syracuse, M. (Gift of the publishers.)
Atlantic monthly, Boston, M.
Babyhood, New York, M.
Century magazine, New York, M.
Chautauquan, Meadville, Pa., M.

Cosmopolitan, New York, M.
Church review, New York, M.
Current literature, New York, M.
Eclectic magazine, New York, M.
Education, Boston, M.
Etude, Philadelphia, M.
Forum, New York, M.
Harper's monthly, New York, M.
Harper's young people, New York, W.
Journal of american folk-lore, Boston, Q.
Journal of comparative medicine, New York, Q.
Journal of morphology, Boston, Irr.
Journal of the Franklin institute, Philadelphia, M.
Lippincott's magazine, Philadelphia, M.
Littell's living age, Boston, W.
Magazine of American History, New York, M.
Magazine of western history, New York, M.
New England historical and genealogical register, Boston, Q.
North American review, New York, M.
Official gazette of the U. S. patent office, Washington, W. (Gift of the
    patent office.)
Outing, New York, M.
Overland monthly, San Francisco, M.
Political science quarterly, Boston, Q.
Popular science monthly, New York, M.
Quarterly journal of economics, Boston, Q.
Railroad and engineering journal, New York, M.
Queries, Buffalo, M.
St. Nicholas, New York, M.
Sanitarian, New York, M.
Science, New York, W.
Scientific American, New York, W.
Scientific American supplement, New York, W.
Scribner's magazine, New York, M.
Swiss cross, New York, M.
Unitarian review, Boston, M. (Gift of the publishers.)
Wide awake, Boston, M.

FRANCE AND ITALY.

Revue des deux mondes, Paris, SM.
Revue internationale, Rome, SM.

GERMANY.

Deutsche revue, Berlin, M.
Deutsche rundschau, Berlin, M.
Geographische mittheilungen, Gotha, M.
Nord und süd, Breslau, M.
Salon, Leipzig, M.
Unsere zeit, Leipzig, M.
Vom fels zum meer, Stuttgart, M.
Westermann's monatshefte, Brunswick, M.

GREAT BRITAIN AND IRELAND.

All the year round, London, W.
Blackwood's Edinburgh magazine, Edinburgh, M.
Chambers's journal, Edinburgh, M.
Contemporary review, London, M.
Cornhill magazine, London, M.
Dublin review, Dublin, Q.
Edinburgh review, Edinburgh, Q.
English historical review, London, Q.
English illustrated magazine, London, M.
Fortnightly review, London, M.
Geographical society's proceedings, London, M.
Good words, London, M.
London society, London, M.
Longman's magazine, London, M.
Macmillan's magazine, London, M.
Murray's magazine, London, M.
Nature, London, W.
Nineteenth century, London, M.
Observatory, London, M.
Quarterly review, London, Q.
Scottisch review, London, Q.
Temple bar, London, M.
Westminster review, London, Q.

IN THE REFERENCE ROOM.

Art amateur, New York, M.
Art journal, New York, M.
Magazine of art, London, M.
Portfolio, London, M.

IN THE LIBRARIAN'S ROOM.

Allgemeine bibliographie für Deutschland, Leipzig, W.

American notes and queries, Philadelphia, W.

Antiquary, London, M.

Appleton's literary bulletin, New York, M. (Gift of the publishers.)

Author, Boston, M.

Book buyer, New York, M.

Book chat, New York, M.

Bookfiend, Minneapolis, M.

Bookmart, Pittsburgh, M.

Book prices current, London, M.

Book worm, London, M.

Centralblatt für bibliothekswesen, Leipzig, M.

Critic, New York, W.

Deutsche literaturzeitung, Berlin, W.

Hinrichs' Bücherverzeichniss, Leipzig. Q. and SA.

Insect life, Washington, M. (Gift of the Department of agriculture.)

Johns Hopkins university circulars, Baltimore, M. (Gift of the pubs.)

Library, London, M.

Library journal, New York, M.

Library notes, Boston, Q.

Literary news, New York, M.

Literary world, Boston, SM.

Literarischer merkur, Leipzig, SM.

Livre, Le, Paris, M.

Notes and queries, London, W.

Publishers' circular, London, SM.

Publishers' weekly, N. Y., W.

Torch and colonial book circular, London, Q.

U. S. government publications monthly catalogue, Wash., M.

Writer, Boston, M.

Zeitschrift für vergleichende literaturgeschichte, Berlin, BM.

Explanation of abbreviations used to denote frequency of publication: SD—twice a day; D—daily; W—weekly: SW—twice a week; BW—every two weeks; SM—twice a month; M—monthly; BM—every two months; Q—four times a year; SA—twice a year.

ACTS OF THE WISCONSIN LEGISLATURE RELATING TO THE PUBLIC LIBRARY.

LAWS OF 1878—CHAPTER 6.

AN ACT relating to the Young Men's Association of the city of Milwaukee, and amendatory of chapter 97 of the laws of 1852.

The people of the State of Wisconsin, represented in senate and assembly, do enact as follows :

SECTION 1. The board of directors of the Young Men's Association of the city of Milwaukee are hereby authorized and empowered, in the name and behalf of said association, to assign, transfer and convey to the city of Milwaukee, all and singular, the books, cabinets, library, furniture, apparatus, fixtures and other property of whatsoever nature, belonging to said association, in trust, to be kept, supported and maintained by said city as a free public library, for the benefit and use of all the citizens of said city, *provided*, the said city shall accept the trust and assume the care and maintenance of such library.

SEC. 2. Before making such transfer and conveyance, the said board of directors shall pay, or provide for paying, all the known debts and liabilities of said association, and with and upon the completed conveyance, transfer and delivery of said property by said board, and its acceptance and assumption by said city, the said Young Men's Association shall be deemed to be dissolved, and its franchise, as a corporation, to be surrendered to the state; *provided*, the power of the present board of directors shall be continued for six months from the date of the passage of this act, for the sole purpose of winding up the affairs and settling the concerns of said association.

SEC. 3. This act shall take effect and be in force from and after its passage.

Approved February 7, 1878.

LAWS OF 1878—CHAPTER 7.

AN ACT to establish and maintain a public library in the city of Milwaukee, (*as amended*).

The people of the State of Wisconsin, represented in senate and assembly, do enact as follows:

SECTION 1. The city of Milwaukee is hereby authorized to establish and maintain a public library therein, for the free use of the inhabitants thereof, and to receive, hold and manage any devise, bequest or donation for the establishment, increase and maintenance of such library under such regulations as are herein contained, or as may hereafter be adopted, as provided in this act.

SEC. 2. The public library, established under this act, shall be considered a branch of the educational department of the city of Milwaukee, and shall be under the general management, control and supervision of a board, consisting of nine members, who shall be styled, "The Board of Trustees of the Public Library of the city of Milwaukee."

SEC. 3. The president of the school board, and the superintendent of public schools of said city, shall be ex-officio members of said board of trustees. William Frankfurth, Gustave C. Trumpff, Matthew Keenan and John

Johnston, residents and taxpayers of the city of Milwaukee, and three members of the common council of said city, to be appointed as hereinafter provided, together with said president of the school board, and said superintendent of public schools, shall be, and are hereby constituted, the first board of trustees. The four trustees above designated by name shall serve for one, two, three and four years from the date of the organization of said board, so that the term of one of them shall expire each year. The respective terms of these four trustees shall be determined by lot at the first meeting of said board after the passage of this act, and their places shall be filled, whenever a vacancy shall occur, by election by the board, from among the citizens at large, and annually, upon the expiration of the term of any such designated trustee, the board shall, at their annual meeting, elect from among the citizens and tax payers of said city, his successor, to serve for the term of four years. [The first three members from the common council shall be appointed by the mayor of said city, at the first meeting of the council held for organization after the charter election in 1878, from the members of the common council, to-wit: one from the three year class of aldermen, one from the two year class of aldermen, and one from the one year class of aldermen, who shall serve as such trustees during their respective terms as such aldermen. And annually, on the third Tuesday in April thereafter, at the expiration of the term of any such trustee, the mayor shall appoint his successor for the term of three years, from the aldermen then having three years to serve. In case any person so appointed trustee shall vacate the office of alderman before the expiration of his term, he shall at the same time cease to be a member of said board of trustees, and the mayor shall appoint some other alderman of his class in his place for the balance of his term.*] None of the said trustees shall receive any compensation from the city treasurer, or otherwise, for their services as such trustees. And no member of said board of trustees shall become, or cause himself to become interested, directly or indirectly, in any contract or job for the purchase of books, pamphlets or other matter pertaining to the library, or of fuel, furniture, stationery or things necessary for the increase and maintenance of the library.

Sec. 4. The first annual meeting of the board of trustees shall be held on the sixth day of May, 1878, at which meeting the board shall organize, by the choice of one of their number as president, to serve for one year, and until his successor shall have been chosen. And it shall be the duty of the city clerk of said city, as soon as practicable after the appointment of the three trustees to be selected from the common council, to give at least three days' notice, in writing, of such meeting of organization, to be held at the office of said city clerk on the said sixth day of May, 1878, to every member of said board. And all subsequent annual meetings of said board shall be held on the second Monday of May in each year, at which a president shall be chosen from their number, to serve for one year, and until his successor shall be chosen.

Sec. 5. The board of trustees shall have general care, control and supervision of the public library, its appurtenances, fixtures and furniture, and of the selection and purchase of books, pamphlets, maps, and other matters appertaining to a public library; and also of the disbursement of all moneys appropriated for and belonging to the library fund, in the manner hereinafter provided. And said board shall adopt, and at their discretion modify,

---

*See amendment, Laws of 1887, page 55 of this report.

amend or repeal by-laws, rules and regulations for the management, care and use of the public library, and fix and enforce penalties for their violation, and generally shall adopt such measures as shall promote the public utility of the library; *provided*, that such by-laws, rules and regulations shall not conflict with the provisions of this act.

SEC. 6. (*As amended by chapter 152, laws of* 1879). The board of trustees shall, at their first meeting, on the sixth day of May, 1878, or thereafter as soon as practicable, and every five years thereafter, at an annual meeting, elect by ballot a person of suitable learning, ability and experience for librarian, who shall also act and be ex-officio secretary of said board of trustees, who shall hold his office for five years from the time of said first annual meeting, unless previously removed, and who shall receive such compensation as may be hereafter fixed by the said board of trustees. And said board of trustees shall also appoint such assistants and employes for said library as they may deem necessary and expedient, and shall fix their compensation. All vacancies in the office of librarian, assistants or other employes, shall be filled by said board of trustees, and the person so selected or appointed shall hold for the unexpired term.

SEC. 7. The librarian elected under this act may be removed from office for misdemeanor, incompetency or inattention to the duties of his office, by a vote of two-thirds of the board of trustees; the assistants and other employes may be removed by the board for incompetency, or for any other cause.

SEC. 8. (*As amended by chapter 152, laws of* 1879). It shall be the duty of the board of trustees, within ten days after the appointment of the librarian and other salaried employes, to report and file with the city comptroller, a duly certified list of the persons so appointed, with the salary allowed to each, and the time or times fixed for the payment thereof, and they shall also furnish such comptroller with a list of all accounts and bills which may be allowed by said board of trustees, stating the character of the materials or service for which the same were rendered, immediately after the meeting of said board, at which such allowance shall be made. And said board of trustees shall also, on or before first the day of October in each year, make to the common council a report, made up to and including the 31st day of August of the said year, containing a statement of the condition of the library, the number of books added thereto, the number of books circulated, and the number of books not returned or lost, together with such information or suggestions as they may deem important: and this report shall contain an account of the moneys credited to the library fund, and expended on account of the same during the preceding year.

SEC. 9. (*As amended by chapter* 152, *laws of* 1879, *and chapter* 60, *laws of* 1882.) The common council shall levy and collect annually upon all taxable property in said city, at the same time and in the same manner as other city taxes are levied and collected by law, a special tax of one-fourth of a mill upon each dollar of the assessed value of said taxable property, and the entire amount of said special tax shall be paid into and held in the city treasury as a separate and distinct fund, to be known as the "library fund", and the same shall not be used or appropriated, directly or indirectly, for any other purpose than for the maintenance and increase of the public library, the payment of the salaries of the librarian, assistants and other employes of the library, the purchase of books, furniture, supplies and fuel, the expenses of rent and insurance, and the incidental expenses, including incidental repairs of the library rooms and furniture.

SEC. 10. (*As amended by chapter* 152 *laws of* 1879.) The board of trustees shall erect, purchase, hire or lease buildings, lots, rooms and furniture for the use and accommodation of said public library, and shall improve, enlarge and repair such library buildings, rooms and furniture; but no lot or building shall be purchased, or erected, or enlarged for the purpose herein mentioned, without an ordinance or resolution of the common council of said city, and deeds of conveyance and leases shall run to the city of Milwaukee.

SEC. 11. All moneys received by, or raised in, the city of Milwaukee for library purposes shall be paid over to the city treasurer, to be disbursed by him on the orders of the president and secretary of the board of trustees, countersigned by the city comptroller. Such order shall be made payable to the order of the persons in whose favor they shall have been issued, and shall be the only vouchers of the city treasurer for the payments from the library fund. The said board of trustees shall provide for the purchase of books, supplies, fuel and other matters necessary for the maintenance of the library; *provided, however,* that it shall not be lawful for said board of trustees to expend or contract a liability for any sum in excess of the amount levied in any one year for the library fund on account of such fund.

SEC. 12. In case the Young Men's Association of the city of Milwaukee shall donate or transfer to the city of Milwaukee its library, fixtures, furniture and other property for the purposes of a free public library, it shall be lawful for said city to accept such donation and transfer, and the board of trustees herein created shall assume the charge and control of said property. It shall also be lawful for said city to receive money, books and other property by devise, bequest or gift from any person or corporation, for library purposes, and to employ or invest the same for the use and benefit of the public library, so far as practicable, iu conformity with the conditions and terms of such devise, bequest or gift.

SEC. 13. In case said Young Men's Association shall make the transfer and donation mentioned in the preceding section, and said city shall accept the same before the date of the annual meeting in May, 1878, as provided in this act, then immediately upon such transfer and acceptance it shall be the duty of the mayor to appoint three aldermen, who, together with the trustees hereinbefore designated by name, and the president of the school board of said city, and the superintendent of public schools, shall constitute a temporary board of trustees, who, until the time of such annual meeting, shall be clothed with all the powers and responsibilities hereinbefore provided, and shall assume the charge, control and management of the property thus donated and accepted, and shall hold and manage the same as provided in this act.

SEC. 14. This act shall take effect and be in force from and after its passage and publication.

Approved February 7, 1878.

LAWS OF 1879—CHAPTER 152.

AN ACT to amend an act entitled an act to establish and maintain a public library in tHe city of Milwaukee, approved February 7, 1878.

The people of the state of Wisconsin, represented in senate and assembly, do enact as follows:

SEC. 4. All moneys, books and other property received by the city of Milwaukee by devise, bequest or gift from any person or corporation, for library purposes, shall, unless otherwise directed by the donors, be under the management and control of said board of trustees; and all moneys derived from fines and penalties for violations of the rules of the library, or from any other source, in the course of the administration of the library, including all moneys which may be paid to the city upon any policy or policies of insurance or other obligation of liability for or on account of loss or damage to any property pertaining to the library, shall belong to the "library fund" in the city treasury, to be disbursed on the orders of said board of trustees, countersigned by the city comptroller, for library purposes, in addition to the amount levied and raised by taxation for such fund.

SEC. 6. This act shall take effect and be in force from and after its passage and publication.

Approved March 1, 1879.

LAWS OF 1887—CHAPTER 521.

AN ACT to amend......chapter 7, of the laws of 1878, to establish a public library in the city of Milwaukee.

The people of the state of Wisconsin, represented in senate and assembly, do enact as follows:

SEC. 1. Hereafter all appointments of members from the common council of the board of trustees of the public library of the city of Milwaukee, made by the mayor on the third Tuesday in April, shall be made from aldermen having two years to serve, and in case any person so appointed shall vacate his office of alderman before the expiration of his term, he shall thereupon cease to be a member of said board of trustees, and the mayor shall appoint some other alderman of his class in his place, to be such trustee for the remainder of his term. Each alderman appointed shall serve as such trustee during his term as alderman. It shall be the duty of the mayor, on the third Tuesday in April in each year, to appoint a sufficient number of aldermen having two years to serve as aldermen, to be members of such board of trustees, to keep the number of members of such board from the common council always three. All provisions of chapter 7 of the laws of 1878 which in any way conflict with the foregoing provisions of this section are hereby amended accordingly.

Approved April 14, 1887.

BY-LAWS OF THE BOARD OF TRUSTEES.

MEETINGS.

ARTICLE 1. The regular meetings of the board shall be held at the library rooms, on the second Tuesday of each month, at 7:30 P. M., except the annual meeting, which shall be held on the second Monday of May.

ART. 2. Special meetings shall be called by the secretary, upon the written request of the president, or any three members of the board; but the object for which the special meeting is held must be stated in the notice, and no business other than the special business shall be transacted at such meeting unless all the members of the board are present and unanimous consent is obtained.

ART. 3. Five members shall constitute a quorum for the transaction of business; but no appropriation shall be made or indebtedness contracted to an amount exceeding $100 without the concurring votes of a majority of all the members of the board.

ART. 4. The order of business of the board of trustees, except at special meetings, shall be as follows:

1. Calling the roll.
2. Reading minutes of previous meeting.
3. Report of librarian and secretary.
4. Report of standing committees.
5. Report of special committees.
6. Reading of communications.
7. Unfinished business.

8. Election of officers.

9. New business.

ART. 5. The records of the proceedings of the board of trustees and its committees shall be kept in the secretary's office, and shall be open at all times to inspection and examination by any member of the board.

ART. 6. The by-laws and rules of the board may be temporarily suspended by unanimous consent of all members present; but no permanent alteration or amendment shall be acted upon until the next regular meeting after the same shall have been proposed, unless each member of the board has been supplied with written copies of the proposed changes at least one week before the meeting of the board.

ART. 7. The rules of parliamentary practice comprised in Robert's Rules of Order shall govern the proceedings of the board in all cases to which they are applicable, and in which they do not conflict with these by-laws, rules and regulations.

OFFICERS.

ART. 8. At the annual meeting in May the board shall elect by ballot a president, whose duty it shall be to preside at all meetings of the board,—to sign all warrants drawn on the city treasurer by order of the board,—to appoint the standing committees for the year,—to prepare, for the consideration and approval of the board, the annual report of the board of trustees, required by the eighth section of the Public Library act,—and otherwise perform all duties incident to his office.

ART. 9. In the temporary absence, or other inability of the president to perform his duties, the board shall elect one of their number president pro tempore.

ART. 10. The duties of the librarian, elected under the provisions of the sixth article of the Public Library act shall be as follows:—to take charge of the library and reading room, and he shall be responsible for the care and safety of the books and other public property contained therein;—to submit to the board of trustees, and to the proper committees, measures for securing the proper management and fullest efficiency of the library and reading room;—to obtain for the library public documents of all kinds, as well as the publication of libraries, library associations, and other bodies, whose proceedings and reports may afford information of value to the board or the users of the library;—to keep carefully arranged, for the use of the board, lists of new books and publications, both American and foreign;—to prepare for the use of the board list of books and periodicals required to complete sets, to fill out such departments as are deficient, and to supply the place of books which have been lost;—to keep a list of all books or publications donated to the library, stating the name and residence of the donor and the date when received;—to classify and arrange all books and publications as soon as received, and to keep the same catalogued according to such plan or plans as may be approved by the board;—to report promptly all flagrant cases of theft, mutilation or injury of books and periodicals;—to be responsible for the preservation of order in the rooms, and to be present, so far as library business will permit, in the library during library hours, except during the evening;—to exercise control over the library and reading room, and all employes of the board, and to promptly report to the executive committee any delinquency on the part of the employes;—to keep exact and detailed accounts of all moneys received from fines and other sources, and report the same monthly to the board at the regular meeting;—to submit monthly a report of all books added to and loaned by the library;—to prepare and submit to the board an annual report, giving a full account of the working of the library during the year ending and including August 31st, said report to accompany the annual report of the board to the common council;—to discharge such other duties as fall within the province of librarian, and may from time to time be prescribed by the board;—but in the performance of his duties as above specified, no debt or liability of any kind shall be incurred by him without express authority from the board.

ART. 11. It shall be the duty of the librarian, as secretary of the board of trustees, to be present at all meetings of the board and of the committees, and to keep full and correct reports of their proceedings;—to keep books of account in which all the money transactions of the board shall be set forth accurately in detail, and to make out and sign all warrants drawn on the city treasurer by order of the board;—to take care of all business papers of the board, and to keep the same neatly filed for convenient reference;—to prepare and submit in his monthly report a statement of the finances of the library;—to give notice of all meetings of the board, and of committees, at least twenty-four hours before the time of meeting;—to transact all such other business as may be required of him by the board and its committees.

ART. 12. The librarian shall be required to give bonds, with two or more sureties, in the sum of $3,000, for the faithful performance of his duties, to be approved by the board and filed with the city comptroller.

ART. 13. For all fines, security deposits and other payments to the library, the librarian shall give his receipt in such form as to show the amount received, in duplicate, one part to be given to the payer and the other kept at the library for permanent reference,—and no claim for undue charges shall be considered by the board, unless the proper receipt shall be submitted in evidence.

ART. 14. All funds received from time to time as fines for overdue books, through sales of catalogues or bulletins, and from all other sources, except security deposits for the safe return of library property, shall be paid by the librarian into the treasury, for the credit of the library fund, at the end of each quarter of the fiscal year of the library.

ART. 15. The board shall elect, from among the regular employes of the library, a suitable person as deputy librarian, who shall exercise the powers and perform the duties of the librarian in his absense or other inability.

ART. 16. In case of a vacancy in the office of president, secretary, or the elected members of the board, such vacancy shall be filled by an election at any regular meeting, or at a special meeting called for that purpose.

COMMITTEES.

ART. 17. The standing committees of the board shall be, (1) the executive committee, (2) the committee on library and reading room, (3) the committee on finance and auditing, (4) the committee on library service. Each of these committees, with the exception of the committee on library service, shall consist of three members, the president being, ex-officio, a member of the executive committee.

ART. 18. The executive committee shall have supervision of all matters relating to the construction, leasing, repairing and furnishing of the rooms or building occupied by the library,—of insuring its property,—and of the order and cleanliness of its rooms.

ART. 19. The committee on library and reading rooms shall have supervision of all matters relating to the selection, purchase and binding of books, periodicals and pamphlets,—the exchange or sale of duplicate or other books,—the arrangement and classification of books,—their preparation for use,—their use and circulation,—their withdrawal from circulation,—the acceptance or rejection of donations,—and the preparation, printing and distribution or sale of catalogues; *provided*, that in all such matters no action shall be taken by the committee until approved by the board. All questions relating to the regulations governing the use of the library, and any proposed addition or amendment thereto, shall be referred to this committee before action is taken by the board.

ART. 20. The committee on finance and auditing shall have supervision of all matters relating to the accounts and account books of the library. It shall be their duty to prepare the annual budget of the board,—to direct the manner of keeping and to examine the account books of the library,—to examine the monthly and other financial statements of the librarian and secretary, and certify to the correctness of the same,—to examine and audit all vouchers and accounts against the library,—and make such suggestions, from time to time, concerning the finances of the library, as they may deem advisable.

ART. 21. A majority of any committee shall constitute a quorum, for the transaction of business under its supervision or referred to it.

ART. 22. It shall be the duty of the several committees to hold monthly meetings, for the purpose of acting upon the matters belonging or referred to them respectively, at such times as each committee may determine for itself, and due notice of every such meeting shall be given to the members of the committee by the secretary. A special meeting of a committee may be called by any member thereof, and at least twenty-four hours' previous notice shall be given, in writing, to the members of the committee by the secretary, stating the object of such meeting.

ART. 23. All reports shall be written and signed by the proper committee. All resolutions shall be in writing, and, if required by any member, motions shall be reduced to writing before being acted upon by the board.

LIBRARY SERVICE.

ART. 24. All applications for permanent positions as assistants in the public library shall be referred to a committee, to be called the committee on library service, and to consist of four members of the board and the librarian. This committee, in determiniug the fitness of candidates for employment by the board, and in recommending appointments, shall be governed by the following rules:

ART. 25. Every application for regular appointment in the public library, together with recommendatiuns, if any, relating to such application, shall be kept on file by the secretary in a separate envelope, and in such form as shall exhibit to members of the board the full name, address, age, place of birth, education, and present or past occupation of the applicant.

ART. 26. It shall be the duty of the librarian, under direction of the committee, to examine, at such time and place as shall be publicly announced in the local press, candidates making application as required in the preceding article. Questions for this examination shall be submitted for the approval of the committee on library service, or of any of its members that shall be selected by said committee.

ART. 27. The examination of all candidates shall be conducted in writing, and shall include such questions as shall test the general knowledge of the applicants, their ability to use the English language correctly in conversation and composition, and their knowledge of such branches as are deemed especially useful to persons employed as assistants in the public library.

ART. 28. All examination papers written by applicants shall be designated by a number, and be accompanied by a sealed envelope bearing the same number and containing the full name and address of the writer, and all papers bearing the name of their writers shall be rejected.

ART. 29. The librarian shall examine the papers submitted by applicants and mark the same upon a uniform basis and upon a scale of one hundred. He shall present these papers, with the record of standing and the sealed envelopes containing the key to their·authors, to the committee on library service.

ART. 30. The committee on library service shall open the envelopes and report to the board the result of the examination, and shall further report on the personal qualifications of candidates, their moral character, behavior and bearing, with any other fact, commendatory or otherwise. But, in determining the preference of candidates, no facts connected with the necessities of the applicants, their relationships, religion, politics, or social position, shall be reported by the committee or considered by the board.

ART. 31. All papers, written reports and records of standing of applicants shall be kept on file by the librarian, and shall be open for inspection by responsible persons; but no papers or other documents connected with the examinations shall be taken from the custody of the librarian.

ART. 32. The library board, upon receiving the report of the committee on library service, shall proceed to elect persons to fill vacancies from those candidates having the highest standing in scholarship, as shown by examination, and whose moral character and personal bearing is favorably reported upon by the committee.

ART. 33. All appointments to fill vacancies in the library shall be on three months' trial, after which, upon favorable report by the librarian and action by the board, employes shall be deemed permanently appointed.

RULES GOVERNING EMPLOYES.

ARTICLE 1. The term of service of the deputy librarian and employes of the public library shall be during good behavior, and they shall only be removed for cause, of which the board shall be the exclusive judge.

ART. 2. The librarian and deputy librarian, and all regular employes, not specially detailed for evening service, shall report daily for duty at 8:30 A. M., except on Sundays and legal holidays. An open record of the times of arrival and departure of all employes shall be kept for the inspection of the members of the board, and it shall be the duty of all employes to report daily to the librarian, or such person as he may designate, the exact time in the forenoon, afternoon or evening, at which they begin and cease service.

ART. 3. The length of a day's service shall be eight hours, and the duties of regular employes shall be arranged by the librarian so as to allow, as nearly as possible, equal leisure for meals, and to assign to each an equitable portion of evening work or special service.

ART. 4. The librarian shall report to the board at the regular monthly meeting all written complaints against attendants, charging them with discourtesy or inattention to duty. He shall further report to what extent the time of each and every employe is occupied, the number of days' or hours' absence of each employe, and the cause of absence,—the number of times tardy, and the time lost by tardiness,—and any and all facts regarding the efficiency of persons employed in the library; said report to include also a statement of the absences of the librarian and the deputy librarian.

ART. 5. In cases of absence, other than absence upon the annual vacation granted by the board, the monthly salary of employes shall be diminished in the ratio which the length of absence bears to the number of working days in the month, reckoning eight hours for one day's service; except in cases of absence caused by sickness or death in the family of employes, in which case the deduction shall be one-half the regular salary, determined in the ratio above mentioned.

ART. 6. In making deductions for absences, the salaries of employes who have been absent during any month or part of a month, shall be audited by the finance committee with the librarian, and the action of said committee shall be reported to the board at its next meeting.

ART. 7. All employes of the library shall be subject to suspension by the librarian, for absenting themselves without leave, want of attention to business, unreasonable waste of time, discourtesy to users of the library, or improper behavior generally. Whenever an employe of the library is suspended, the librarian shall immediately report the same to the executive committee, and shall submit to the board at its next regular meeting, a full statement of the matter.

ART. 8. In case of the absence of an employe, where service is urgently needed, the librarian shall have power to employ a suitable person as substitute, at a compensation to be fixed by the executive committee, and report his action to the board, at the next meeting, for consideration and approval.

Art. 9. In the absence of the librarian, the deputy librarian shall assume full management of all matters appertaining to the library and the duties or service of employes.

Art. 10. A copy of these rules for the government of employes in the library shall be printed and hung in such place in the reading room, reference department and issuing department, as shall be convenient for perusal by the public and by employes.

RULES GOVERNING DELIVERY STATIONS.

Art. 1. For the benefit of residents of the city living at a distance from the library, the board shall maintain three or more distributing stations for the delivery of books to persons who are entitled to the privileges of the library, and have complied with the requirements made and provided for the drawing of books. The stations shall be located by the committee on library and reading room, subject to approval by the board. They shall be situated as far as practicable, at such points as will accommodate the largest number of residents living in parts of the city from which the library is not conveniently accessible. They shall be selected with a view to agreeableness and quietness of surroundings, and admit of being freely visited by adults and youth of both sexes.

Art. 2. The person in charge of the premises where books are distributed, shall receive a compensation for the care of library property and for services performed, the amount of such compensation to be determined by the library committee and approved by the board. Such person or persons shall sign the following agreement, which shall be submitted to and accepted by the board in each case, viz:

I, ..., hereby agree to perform the duties of distributing agent for the board of trustees of the Milwaukee Public Library for the period of .... from the date hereof, in accordance with the rules prescribed by said board; and for all services performed as such agent, I hereby agree to accept the sum total of $...... per month, which amount shall include all claims made by me against said library board for rent of room or space in which to deposit library property, and books awaiting delivery or return to the library.

ART. 3. Distributing agents shall deliver books to cardholders, and receive books, cards and lists in application for books, between 9 A. M. and 8 P. M. of all days during which their places of business are open to the public.

They shall wait upon book borrowers with as much promptness as circumstances will permit,—keep in sight and convenient for public use such catalogues and notices as the library board shall supply for the purpose,—exercise vigilance in the care of property belonging to the library, and see that book borrowers are courteously treated and accommodated in all reasonable requests for books and information respecting the use of the library.

ART. 4. Distributing agents shall obey fully and promptly any request of the librarian in regard to the retention or return to the library of any and all books or property, and shall make such reports as to the condition or number of books on hand, or as to the condition of any library property, and shall give such information concerning the same as the librarian may request.

ART. 5. It shall be the duty of the distributing agent

to receive books delivered from the library,—to place and secure the same in repositories provided for the purpose by the library board,—to pack ready for immediate transfer to the library at the call of the carrier all books and cards left at the station by borrowers,—to notify the librarian immediately of any loss of property belonging to the ibrary or damage to the same,—and generally to assist in promoting the interests of the public and the usefulness of the library.

ART. 6. The committee on library and reading room shall engage a responsible person, acceptable to the board, and at a compensation approved by the board, to transfer books and other property between the library and the distributing stations. The frequency of delivery of book packages shall be regulated by special act of the board, but not less than one delivery a day shall be made for a period of six months from the adoption of these rules.

ART. 7. The committee on library shall have general charge of the delivery station system and shall report to the board at the regular monthly meeting all matters of importance relating thereto, and make such recommendations as they deem necessary to sustain and increase the efficiency of this department of the library service.

ART. 8. The librarian shall keep a separate account of each delivery station, specifying the number and classes of all books distributed through each agency, as required in Art. 5 of these rules, and at the regular monthly meeting of the board, and in his annual report, he shall enter separately and distinctly the statistics of the distribution of each station, with such other facts as he may deem of interest to the public and of importance to the board.

ART. 9. These rules shall be printed, and a copy furnished each of the station keepers, for posting in a conspicuous place.

REGULATIONS.

ARTICLE 1. The library shall be open on all secular days from 9 o'clock A. M. to half-past 8 o'clock P. M. The reading rooms shall be open from the same hour to 9 o'clock P. M.

ART. 2. Any person of good deportment and habits may use the reading room. The use of tobacco, and all conversation, and other conduct not consistent with the quiet and orderly use of the reading room, are prohibited.

ART. 3. Any resident of Milwaukee may draw books from the library by signing an agreement to observe all the rules and regulations of the library and complying with either of the following conditions:

1. Giving satisfactory security in the form following:

Milwaukee,...................................18...

I, the subscriber, hereby certify that...............................
residing at No.....................................Street, is a fit person
to enjoy the privileges of the Milwaukee Public Library,
and for value received, I agree that I will be responsible for
the observance by.............of the regulations of the library,
and will make good any injury or loss the library may sus-
tain from or by reason of the permission to draw books
that may be given in consequence of this certificate.

(Signed)...
Residing at No.........................Street.

"N. B.—The privileges granted in consequence of this certificate shall terminate at the end of two years from its date and may be sooner revoked, at pleasure, by the librarian or board of trustees of the library, or by the signer."

2. Depositing three dollars, and, in special cases, such further sum as the value of the book asked for may, in the judgment of the librarian, require. For such deposits receipts shall be given.

ART. 4. Each person entitled to draw books from the library will be supplied with a card, inscribed with his or her name, residence and register number. This card must be produced whenever a book is taken, returned or renewed. *Immediate notice of a change of residence must be given at the library.* Neglect to give this notice will subject the card-holder to foreiture of privileges.

ART. 5. The holder of a card is entitled to draw one volume if octavo or larger size; or two volumes of smaller size than octavo, they being the same work.

ART. 6. Books may be retained two weeks, and may be once renewed for the same period. Application for renewal must be made within the first fourteen days.

ART. 7. Books of recent purchase, labeled "Seven Day Book," cannot be retained more than one week and cannot be renewed.

ART. 8. Encyclopedias, dictionaries and other works of reference, elaborately illustrated books, and such others as may be unsuited for general circulation, can be used only in the reference room.

ART. 9. A fine of three cents a day shall be paid on each volume which is not returned according to the provisions of the preceding rules; and no book will be delivered to the party incurring the fine till it is paid.

Art. 10. Writing in books is prohibited; and all injuries to books, beyond reasonable wear, and all losses, shall be promptly adjusted to the satisfaction of the librarian.

Art. 11. Delinquents will be notified through the mail, on the third day after their delinquency has occurred; and one week thereafter, if the book is not returned, the guarantor will be notified. If the book is not returned within twenty days after serving the first notice, the librarian shall proceed to collect, through the law department of the city, the value of the book, with accrued fines and other charges to the date of payment.

Art. 12. Any person abusing the privileges of the library, or violating these regulations, shall be temporarily suspended from the use of the library, and the case shall be reported to the library committee for proper action thereon.

Art. 12. The library cards of persons by whom fines or charges have been or shall be incurred, and who shall neglect to pay such fines or charges within thirty days after they were incurred, shall be canceled by the librarian; and no card shall be issued by any such delinquent until all such fines and charges shall have been paid.

Art. 14. The written certificate or guaranty, furnished under Art. 3, shall only entitle the person for whom it is given, to the privileges of the library for two years from its date, or until sooner revoked by the librarian, the board of trustees of the library, or by the signer of such certificate. And upon the expiration of such two years, or upon such revocation, the card of the book-borrower shall be surrendered and canceled, and no further book shall be delivered to him or her, until new and satisfactory security shall be given under said Art. 3.

Art. 15. In case of the loss of a borrower's card, immediate notice thereof must be given to the librarian, and, upon application, a duplicate card may be issued to the borrower, upon the payment of a fine of ten cents.

Art. 16. The drawing of books through the various distributing stations, established by the board of trustees, shall be governed by the same regulations as prescribed for the use of the general library. Blanks for the agreement and guaranty stipulated in Art. 3 will be furnished by the agent at each station, who will transmit them, when properly filled out, to the librarian. Fines imposed for delinquencies may be paid to the agent for transmission to the library, at the same time as the book is returned, or at any other time, but any error made by the agent in the calculation of fines will be corrected by the librarian, and must be settled before another book is issued.

General Law of the State of Wisconsin for the Protection of Public Libraries.

LAWS OF 1875—CHAPTER 270.

AN ACT to protect public libraries, and the libraries of literary, scientific, historical and library associations and societies.

The people of the State of Wisconsin, represented in senate and assembly, do enact as follows :

SECTION 1. Any person who shall willfully, maliciously or wantonly tear, deface or mutilate, or by other means injure any book, pamphlet, map, chart, painting or picture belonging to any public library, or to any library, the property of any literary, scientific, historical or library society or association, whether incorporated or unincorporated, shall be deemed guilty of a misdemeanor, and, on conviction thereof, shall be punished by a fine of not less than five dollars, nor more than one hundred dollars, or by imprisonment in the county jail of not less than ten nor more than sixty days, in the discretion of the court; and all justices of the peace in their respective counties shall have jurisdiction to hear, try and determine all prosecutions under this act.

SEC. 2. Any person who shall procure or take, in any way whatever, from the library of any public library, or library of any literary, scientific, historical or library society or association whatever, incorporated or not, any book, pamphlet, map, chart, painting or picture, with intent to convert the same to his own use, or who shall convert the same to his own use with intent to defraud the owner thereof, shall be punished by a fine of not less than ten nor more than one hundred dollars, or, in the discretion of the court, by imprisonment in the county jail for not more than three months.

SEC. 3. It shall be the duty of every librarian, board of trustees, directors or other officers or persons having charge or control of any such library as is mentioned in this act, to post up, in one or more conspicuous place in the room or rooms where the same shall be kept, a printed copy of this act.

SEC. 4. This act shall take effect and be in force from and after its passage and publication.

Approved March 5, 1875.

CONTENTS.

THIRTEENTH

ANNUAL * REPORT

— OF THE —

Board of Trustees

— OF THE —

PUBLIC

Library

OF THE CITY OF

MILWAUKEE.

October 1, 1890,

STANDARD PRINTING CO., 114 MICHIGAN ST.,
MILWAUKEE

THIRTEENTH

ANNUAL REPORT

OF THE

BOARD OF TRUSTEES

OF THE

PUBLIC · LIBRARY

OF THE

CITY OF MILWAUKEE.

_____

OCTOBER 1ST, 1890.

_____

MILWAUKEE.
STANDARD PRINTING COMPANY,
1891.

LIBRARY SERVICE.

KLAS AUGUST LINDERFELT, Librarian and Secretary.
MARY ELVA STILWELL, Amanuensis.

CATALOGUING AND REFERENCE DEPARTMENTS.
THERESA HUBBELL WEST, Sup't and Deputy Librarian.
WILLY SCHMIDT, Assistant.
WILLIAM JOHN KERSHAW, Evening Attendant.

ISSUING DEPARTMENT.
LUTIE EUGENIA STEARNS, Superintendent.
EVA SHEAFE COE, Assistant.
BELLE BLEND, Assistant.
KARIN SCHUMACHER, Assistant.
FRED LAU, Assistant.
EDWARD ALDEN DONALDSON, Evening Assistant.
JOSEPHINE BUNTESCHU, Extra Assistant.

READING ROOMS.
HARRIET ISABELLE WHITE, Superintendent.
AGNES SULLIVAN, Assistant.

JANITOR.
HEINRICH SCHWARTZ.

NIGHT WATCHMAN.
DAVID EDWARD DALE.

REPORT OF THE BOARD OF TRUSTEES.

To the Common Council of the City of Milwaukee:

GENTLEMEN:

In accordance with the provisions of the law for the establishment of a public library in the city of Milwaukee, the Board of Trustees herewith submits its thirteenth annual report, and refers, in so doing, for a detailed account of the work accomplished by the library during the past year, and of other matters pertaining to the administration, to the accompanying report of the librarian.

The growth of the library in our charge continues to be steady, both as regards the accumulation of books and the increased use made of the same by all classes of the inhabitants of the city. It has constantly been the aim of the Board of Trustees to facilitate in every way the drawing of books, consistent with the necessary safeguards for their proper return in due season, and unceasing efforts have been made to promote the wide diffusion of healthy literature, offered by the library, to the exclusion of the positively bad or merely indifferent, which now-a-days is crowding forward at an astonishingly low price. As an unqualified success in this direction, we wish to call particular attention to the efforts made to put the library in intimate connection with the public schools in all parts of the city, by distributing books to the pupils by their teachers. The statistics of this circulation exhibited in the librarian's report show how far this system has been already developed. It is with great pleasure the Board expresses its appreciation of the promptness of your honorable body in ratifying its choice of a suitable and in every way satisfactory lot for the erection of a public library and museum building. If the city had been searched from one end to the other, it is doubtful whether a better building site could have been secured, and we look forward with confidence to the com·pletion in the near future of a building to accomodate these two educational institutions, which will be an ornament to our city, even when its rapid growth shall have made it much larger than it now is, and beautiful buildings much more numerous along its streets.

For the Board of Trustees of the Milwaukee Public Library,

MATTHEW KEENAN,

President.

REPORT OF THE LIBRARIAN.

MILWAUKEE, October 1st, 1890.

To the Board of Trustees of the Milwaukee Public Library:

GENTLEMEN:—In accordance with your rules for the government of this library, I have the honor to submit herewith my report as librarian and secretary, on the condition and work of the library for the official year ending August 31, 1890, being the thirteenth annual report since the organization of the library.

It is with great pleasure that I record, as the most important fact in the history of the library during the year, the acquisition by the city of an eligible site for the new library-museum building. For the purpose of carrying out the provisions of the act, referred to in my last report, in accordance with the spirit of the acts establishing the library and the museum, the boards of trustees of these two institutions appointed a joint committee to consider and report on such sites as were obtainable for the sum authorized by said act. This committee held its first meeting on January 8, 1890, and after carefully considering the various offers received from property owners in all parts of the city, unanimously agreed on the northeast corner of Grand Avenue and Ninth Street as the most suitable, all things considered. In conformity with this decision, the two boards of trustees recommended to the common council the purchase of four lots and part of a fifth, containing 33,830 square feet, in this locality for the sum of $60.000, and on February 24, 1890, the common council adopted this recommendation. The property has since been transferred to the city and is thus designated to become the location for the permanent home of the public library and the public museum of the city of Milwaukee. It is doubtful, whether another place could have been selected, so eminently suitable for this purpose, situated as it is on high ground, at the beginning of one of the choicest residence portions of the city, on one of its most beautiful streets, and still within a few minutes walk of the business center, while it is almost the exact geographical center of the city within the corporate limits. A good building, commensurate with the needs of the rapidly growing institutions, for which it is designed, erected on this commanding site, will always be a notable feature of the city and testify in no uncertain terms to the fostering care of its citizens for all educational interests and the cause of popular intelligence.

The statistics of library work for the year, following the same arrangement as that employed in previous reports, are as follows:

BOOKS.

The number of bound volumes in the library at the close of last report was 48,655. During the year 4,480 volumes were added, of which number 3,610 volumes were acquired by purchase, 462 volumes consisted of magazines and pamphlets bound and placed permanently on the shelves, and the remaining 408 volumes were given to the library by various persons and institutions, a detailed statement of which will be found in appendix E. During the same time, 338 volumes were worn out and discarded as unserviceable, and 11 volumes were lost and paid for by borrowers. The book account therefore, at the end of the year, stands as follows:

On hand Sept. 1, 1889 ....48,655 vols.

Added up to August 31st, 1890.

By gift as per appendix E .... 408 vols.
By purchase and exchange.....................3,610 "
By transfer by binding............................ 462 "
                —————— 4,480 vols.

Total...53,135 vols.
Deduct books discarded .... 338 vols.
Deduct books lost and paid for...... .... 11 "
                ————— 349 vols.

In the library at the close of the year........................52,786 vols.

The number of unbound pamphlets received during the year, that have not been bound up at once in book form and entered as books, is 486, of which 3 were acquired by purchase, while 483 were given to the library, as per detailed statement in appendix E.

CLASSIFICATION OF ACCESSIONS.

The new books added to the library during the year belong to the following classes:

	Volumes.	Percentage.
General and bibliographical works..................	474	10.6
Philosophy and ethics.....................................	55	1.2
Religion and theology..............	119	2.7
Social and political science.............................	364	8.1
Philology..........................	27	.6
Natural science...	482	10.8
Useful arts...........................	259	5.8
Fine arts..	98	2.2
Literature in general............................\..........	170	3.8
Poetry and drama	76	1.7
Prose fiction and children's books..................	1431	31.9
History...	440	9.8
Geography and travels....................................	309	6.9
Biography....................................	176	3.9
	4,480	100.

Owing to the increased demand on the resources of the library for books suitable for young people's reading, by reason of the system of school distribution, detailed in last report, it has been found necessary to provide a large number of duplicates of such books, and not only has the $500 referred to as set apart for this purpose been expended, but a like amount as well, which circumstance will explain the unusually large percentage of this class of literature in the year's purchases.

Of the whole number of books added, 4,254 volumes were in the English, 172 in the German, 47 in the French, and 7 in other languages.

COST OF BOOKS.

The amount expended for books and pamphlets during the year is $5,722.96, which includes $156.23 paid on account of books received during the year embraced in last report. Deducting this amount, and adding $434.08, which was audited and paid after the close of this report, for books counted among the accessions of the year, shows that the actual cost of the books added to the library was $6,000.71.

BINDING.

The number of volumes rebound during the year is 1865, while 227 volumes were resewed and put back in the old covers. During the same period, 367 new books, 131 pamphlets, 565 magazines and newspapers were bound. The total amount paid for this work is $1,190.21, to which, however, must be added $148.28, audited and paid after the close of this report, making the entire cost of the year's binding $1,338.49. Minor repairs on books, as well as labeling and arranging the new books for circulation, have, as usual, been done by the library attendants.

CIRCULATION OF BOOKS.

In appendix A, will be found the usual detailed statement of the aggregate circulation of the library by months, and in appendix B the record of the several delivery stations. This shows that the total number of books taken out for home use during 299 working days was 144,251, being a daily average of 482.4 volumes. The date of largest circulation was March 15, when 829 volumes were issued, which is the highest number of books issued in one day since the establishment of the library; and the smallest, 210 volumes, September 9. The month of highest daily average of issue, 584, was April; and of the lowest, 311, September.

For comparison, I subjoin a statement of the circulation, by months, for the last three years:

MONTHS.	1887–8.		1888–9.		1889–90.	
	Working days.	Volumes issued.	Working days.	Volumes issued.	Working days.	Volumes issued.
September ...	24½	6797	24	6839	24	7464
October	25½	8018	27	8048	27	9731
November....	25	8118	24	8923	25	11832
December.....	25	8425	24	9656	23	11835
January.......	25	9480	26	11341	26	13270
February.....	24	9947	23	11036	23	13040
March.........	27	11160	26	12589	26	15107
April...........	25	9347	25	13378	26	15189
May	26	9684	26	9749	26	13617
June...........	26	7702	25	11387	25	13473
July	25	7185	26	8520	26	9752
August	23	6891	24	7579	22	9941
Total...........	301	102754	300	119045	299	144251
Daily average	341.3		376.8		482.4	

As will be seen from this statement, the total number of books issued for home use is very much larger, than during

the preceding year, the increase averaging more than 100
volumes for each working day. It can hardly be doubted
that this is largely the result of spreading the knowledge
of the library, and the benefits it offers, among all classes
of the inhabitants of the city by means of the books distributed through the public schools. These books go into
almost every household and frequently arouse the desire of
other members of the family to avail themselves of the op-
portunities for instructive or entertaining reading, offered
them for the mere asking. Through the delivery stations
were sent out 18,793 volumes, and through the schools
13,769 volumes while the branch library at Bay View circulated 2390 volumes from its very limited resources. The
number of books given out at the main building is therefore 109,299 volumes, irrespective of the books used or
read within the library rooms, an increase of over 14,000
volumes over the preceding year.

CLASSIFICATION OF CIRCULATION.

The percentages of circulation in the different classes of
literature, for the last four years, are as follows:

	1886-7.	1887-8.	1888-9.	1889-90.
General works	1.4	4.1	4.2	4.8
Philosophy	.8	.7	.7	.6
Theology	.1	1.1	.9	1.1
Social and political science.	1.2	1.3	1.5	1.2
Philology	.1	.2	.1	.1
Natural science	2.	1.7	1.9	3.2
Useful arts	1.7	1.6	1.8	1.7
Fine arts	1.6	1.7	1.5	1.7
Literature in general	6.4	5.7	5.3	6.2
Prose fiction	59.	58.2	56.9	48.2
Children's literature	15.	14.4	14.7	18.9
History	4.	3.6	4.2	5.3
Geography and travels	3.4	3.5	3.9	5.4
Biography	2.4	2.2	2.4	2.6

The steady decrease in the amount of prose fiction drawn from the library, as compared with other books, still continues, and the percentage of this class of literature is now lower than in any other library in the country of the same nature as our own. This gratifying result is directly traceable to the systematic efforts made by the superintendent of the delivery department to guide those, who come to the library without any definite ideas of what they want, in the direction of useful and instructive reading. That such is the case is conclusively shown by a comparison of this table with the exhibit, in appendix B, of the classification of books drawn through the several delivery stations, where no such guidance is possible. The influence of the teachers' selection through the school distribution is seen in the increased percentages of children's literature, natural science, history, and travels.

SCHOOL DISTRIBUTION.

The system of distributing books through the public schools, described in the last report, has been continued throughout the school year and largely extended, until it takes in almost every school in the city. At the solicitation of many teachers, who found six weeks too short a time for keeping the books, before returning them to the library, this period was extended to two months, a change which experience has proved to be decidedly beneficial. Under this arrangement, each class changes its stock of reading matter only four times during the entire school year. The number of books drawn by 97 teachers in 23 schools was 3,863, which were given out 13,769 times, each volume being thus read on an average 3½ times while at the schools. In order to supply the books needed for this work it was found necessary to set aside $500 for the purchase of duplicates of the most desirable works at two different times during the year, and this appropriation must undoubtedly be repeated in the near future.

BOOK BORROWERS AND REGISTRATION.

The number of new registrations during the year was 5,437, making the total number of names registered up to the close of this report 41,278. Of this number, 31,059 cards have been called in from time to time, after running for the designated period of two years, leaving 10,219 cards now nominally in force. For various other causes, such as removal from the city, failure to pay fines, withdrawal of guaranty, etc., 333 cards were canceled during the year. Of the new cards, fourteen were issued in consideration of the stipulated money deposit, and eighteen such deposits were withdrawn, leaving eight deposits still on hand.

READING ROOM.

The total number of visitors to the reading room during the 299 week days it was open, was 66,287, being a daily average of 222, an increase of 26 over the average of the preceding year. On application at the counter, 4,583 magazines were delivered to readers, an average of 15 per day, all other periodicals and papers being kept on tables, open to all comers. On 52 Sunday afternoons, the number of visitors was 5,623, an average attendance of 108, and 683 magazines, or 13 each day, were drawn for reading.

There are now kept on file 235 serial publications, of which 168 are magazines of general interest or for special purposes, and 67 newspapers. The number of magazines is made up of 107 American, 38 English, 4 French, and 19 German publications. The newspapers comprise 24 dailies, 43 weeklies, semi-monthlies and monthlies, representing the United States, Canada, England, Scotland,

Ireland, and Germany. Forty-one newspapers and twelve magazines are furnished to the library free of charge, a detailed statement of which will be found in appendix F. The total amount expended on this department during the year is $867.72, which includes the cost of the extra copies of Harper's Magazine, Century Magazine, Scribner's Magazine, Atlantic Monthly, Lippincott's Magazine, St. Nicholas, Wide Awake, and Harper's Young People, which are furnished borrowers for home use in monthly numbers.

REFERENCE ROOM.

Although largely used during the year, no statistics are available for showing such use, for reasons explained in former reports, except as to the number of readers on Sunday afternoons. These were 1907 on 52 Sundays, being an average of 37 each Sunday, the highest number being 81 in March, and the smallest, 7, in July.

CATALOGUING.

The cataloguing of new accessions has been done by the same force as before, except that the amanuensis added to the library employes has assisted in copying catalogue slips on the typewriter. Four new numbers of the Quarterly Index of Additions have been published during the year, ending with no. 16, and also title and indexes to vol. 2, comprising nos. 9 to 16 inclusive. The cost of this printing, including the binding of 50 copies of vol. 2, was $485.08. The amount received for the sale of catalogues and bulletins is $28.56.

In order to furnish convenient lists of selected books for use as call slips by the numerous borrowers, who require guidance in the choice of their reading matter, two small four-page catalogues have been issued, one containing

"100 of the best English novels, with 50 of the best translations," and the other "150 good books for children," exclusive of novels. These little lists have met with great favor among our reading public, and it seems desirable to continue them with other lists of selections from other departments of the library.

ADMINISTRATION.

The pressure of business, resulting from the greatly increased use of the library, made it necessary to provide, at the beginning of the present calendar year, an amanuensis, skilled in stenography and typewriting, for the assistance of the librarian and the cataloguing department. For this position Miss M. E. Stillwell was selected, after a thorough examination. In other respects the library force remains the same, except that during the busiest months an extra attendant was added in the issuing department. The aggregate amount paid out for salaries of all kinds, but not including those of the keepers of the stations, is $8,340.14.

The cost of maintaining the delivery stations, including the salaries paid to the keepers, and the amount paid the Lightning Messenger and Express Co. for cartage during the year, is $844.11. In June the People's Institute, in whose rooms one of the stations is located, was accorded the privilege of commuting the usual compensation of $5 per month into subscriptions to the best periodicals to the amount of $60 per year at the rates paid by the library, for use in its reading rooms, a change which has been very satisfactory to its patrons, while entailing no extra expense to the library. The periodicals remain the property of the public library, and are returned to it after three months' use.

INSURANCE.

The total insurance carried by the library on its property is $65,000, distributed among the following companies:

Ætna Insurance Co., Hartford.. .....$2,500
Allemannia Fire Insurance Co., Pittsburg....................................... 2,500
Amazon Insurance Co., Cincinnati...................... 2,500
Boatman's Fire and Marine Insurance Co., Pittsburg................. 2,500
British America Assurance Co., Toronto 2,500
Buffalo German Insurance Co.. 2,500
Citizens' Insurance Co., Pittsburg.....................................: 2,500
Concordia Fire Insurance Co., Milwaukee................... 5,000
Fire Insurance Co. of the County of Philadelphia........................ 2,500
German Fire Insurance Co. of Peoria, Ill........... 2,500
Glens Falls Insurance Co., Glens Falls, N. Y.................................. 2,500
Insurance Company of North America, Philadelphia 2,500
Michigan Fire and Marine Insurance Co., Detroit......................... 2,500
Milwaukee Mechanics' Insurance Co.. 5,000
Norwich Union Fire Insurance Society, U. S. Branch, New York... 2,500
Pennsylvania Fire Insurance Co., Philadelphia.............................. 2,500
Queen Insurance Co. of Liverpool, Western Dep't, Chicago.......... 2,500
Rhode Island Underwriters' Association, Providence.................... 2,500
Rochester German Insurance Co... 2,500
Rockford Insurance Co., Rockford, Ill.. 2,500
Security Insurance Co., New Haven 2,500
Sun Fire Office of London, U. S. Branch, Watertown, N. Y........... 2,500
Western Assurance Co., Toronto.. 2,500
Williamsburg City Fire Insurance Co...... 2,500

FINANCIAL REPORT.

In conclusion, I beg leave to submit the usual statement of the receipts and expenditures of the library during the year, including both the miscellaneous receipts of the librarian and the account with the city treasurer, as follows:

CASH ACCOUNT.

RECEIPTS.

Cash on hand September 1, 1889..........................$	58.26
Fines for undue detention of books..........................	409.66
Catalogues sold..	17.05
Builetins sold...	11.51
Security deposits...	42.00
Books lost or damaged...	8.97
Lost cards replaced	15.00

DISBURSEMENTS.

Security deposits refunded...	$	60.00
Refunded for lost books restored...............................		.85
Fines refunded..		.54
Paid city treasurer		330.50
Cash on hand August 31, 1890.................................		170.56
	$562.45	$562.45

LIBRARY FUND ACCOUNT.

DEBIT.

Balance, as per last report................................$	8,794.06	
Paid by the librarian...	330.50	
Appropriation for 1890..............................	25,124.55	
		$34,249.11

CREDIT.

Amount drawn on vouchers issued by your
board during the official year on account of

Rent ....$	1,750.00	
Salaries...	8,340.14	
Fuel and gas..	912.16	
Books...	5,722.96	
Newspapers and periodicals.................................	867.72	
Postage, express and freight...............................	121.31	
Furniture and repairs...	377.02	
Stationery and printing	513.05	
Printing Quarterly additions..............................	485.08	
Insurance	666.25	
Binding	1,190.21	
Delivery stations..	844.11	
Miscellaneous	208.71	
		$21,998.71
Balance in library fund Sept. 1, 1890..........		$12,250.39

All of which is respectfully submittted.

K. A: LINDERFELT,

Librarian and Secretary.

APPENDIX A.
AGGREGATE CIRCULATION.

	Days open.	General works.	Philosophy.	Theology.	Social and Political Science.	Philology.	Natural Science.	Useful Arts.	Fine Arts.	Literature.	Prose fiction.	Children's fiction.	History.	Geography.	Biography.	Total Circulation.	Date and highest circulation.	Date and lowest circulation.	Daily average.	Number of cards issued.	Notices sent.
September, 1889	24	282	67	73	108	10	127	118	122	386	4,509	1,101	226	199	136	7,464	21-545	9-210	311	223	170
October, "	27	367	61	103	135	11	162	138	161	540	5,487	1,695	362	334	169	9,731	12-638	2-258	360	680	170
November, "	25	547	72	134	180	7	243	214	266	789	5,835	2,085	575	619	316	11,832	2-706	1-285	473	646	156
December, "	23	612	54	107	133	9	240	211	230	656	5,647	2,371	622	637	316	11,835	27-772	17-297	515	423	140
January, 1890...	26	648	72	163	164	11	327	225	224	724	6,706	2,324	584	704	394	13,270	25-721	21-291	510	591	114
February, " ...	23	614	72	224	163	8	363	238	274	797	6,057	2,228	717	846	439	13,040	15-764	14-388	567	555	88
March, " ...	26	821	109	185	207	10	366	293	322	779	7,545	2,397	795	797	481	15,107	15-829	28-419	581	591	141
April, " ...	26	785	56	160	180	16	508	262	208	788	6,710	3,189	833	1,077	417	15,189	18-761	17-391	584	460	156
May, " ...	26	642	74	182	192	18	610	242	225	708	6,449	2,491	659	755	375	13,617	10-735	2-373	524	658	187
June, " ...	25	750	52	108	94	6	913	229	158	524	4,846	3,369	1,044	1,102	288	18,478	21-580	24-272	539	209	216
July, " ...	26	414	63	70	107	6	351	170	168	850	4,997	1,948	665	330	178	9,752	19-511	30-260	375	242	253
August, " ...	22	430	50	96	99	8	361	166	149	395	4,781	2,129	673	401	203	9,941	20-719	5-292	452	209	129
TOTAL.........	289	6,912	802	1,600	1,712	115	4,571	2,496	2,502	7,442	69,569	27,322	7,695	7,801	3,712	144,251	829	210	482.4	5,437	1,920
PER CENT......		4.8	.6	1.1	1.2	.1	3.2	1.7	1.7	5.2	48.2	18.9	5.3	5.4	2.6	100					

APPENDIX B.

CIRCULATION OF DELIVERY STATIONS.

A.—SOUTH SIDE, 1st AVENUE.

	Days open	General works	Philosophy	Theology	Social and political science	Philology	Natural science	Useful arts	Fine arts	Literature	Prose fiction	Children's fiction	History	Geography	Biography	Total circulation	Date and highest circulation	Date and lowest circulation	Daily average
September, 1889	25				1		2	2	1	7	121	49	3	3	2	191	18—19	9—1	7
October, "	27			1			1	2	3	6	135	80	5	8	1	242	10—23	4—3	9
November, "	25	1		1			1	3	6	5	122	72	4	3		217	7—19	2—3	9
December, "	23	3		3			6	4	1	13	170	89	3	2	3	281	30—33	31—3	12
January, 1890	26	4			4		8	5	3	19	214	88	6	7	6	351	16—26	27—5	14
February, "	23		5	1	1		6	8	2	12	159	69	16	28	4	323	28—32	20—5	14
March, "	26	1		3	2		1	2	5	14	235	105	5	8		382	29—27	25—7	15
April, "	26	3						1	4	6	228	111	8	9	11	397	5—24	8—8	15
May, "	26	4		1	1		8	5	6	4	240	120	10	9	5	412	7—27	31—7	16
June, "	25	9					7	2	6	5	189	86	19	15	1	343	2—26	17—3	14
July, "	26	9			1		32	6	6	6	156	116	35	13		370	23—27	21—4	14
August, "	22	5		1			23	5	6	10	126	79	37	18	4	303	22—52	9—5	14
Total	300	39	5	11	10		95	43	45	103	2095	1064	151	113	38	3812		52	112.7
Per cent		1.	.1	.3	.3		2.5	1.1	1.2	2.7	54.9	27.9	4.	3.	1.				

CIRCULATION OF DELIVERY STATIONS.—CONTINUED.

B—EAST SIDE.

	Days open.	General works.	Philosophy.	Theology.	Social and political science.	Philology.	Natural science.	Useful arts.	Fine arts.	Literature.	Prose fiction.	Children's fiction.	History.	Geography.	Biography.	Total circulation.	Date and highest circulation.	Date and lowest circulation.	Daily average.
September, 1889	25	4		4	2		6	6		8	159	31	5	5	6	236	27–20	30–5	9
October, "	27	2		4	3		7	10	1	10	181	47	7	2	3	277	30–19	21–2	10
November, "	25	4		3	3		10	4		4	169	23	3	8	2	236	20–16	4–2	9
December, "	23	7	1	9	2			3	3	13	143	30	4	5	3	222	30–27	9–2	10
January, 1890	26	11	1	6			2	5	1	15	160	20	12	15	8	256	14–18	13–2	10
February, "	23	14	1	7	1		4	8	4	10	142	28	12	27	12	268	11–19	17–4	12
March, "	26	4		3	1		1	5	2	17	171	45	11	5	19	298	22–18	25–6	11
April, "	26	12	1	6			1	5	2	10	178	40	2	16	12	284	1–18	14–4	11
May, "	26	9		4	3		1	2	3	11	209	40	9	7	4	303	16–18	12–4	12
June, "	25	4	1	1	2		1	4	1	15	151	24	23	6		233	26–16	25–4	9
July, "	26	5	1		5		8	4	9	14	160	35	31	11	3	286	23–19	21–2	11
August, "	22	7		3	4		6	1	9	14	131	38	18	7		246	22–15	14–2	11
Total	300	93	6	50	26		48	57	36	144	1954	401	137	114	79	3145	45	2	10.4
Per cent.		3.	.2	1.6	.8		1.5	1.8	1.1	4.6	62.1	12.8	4.4	3.6	2.5				

CIRCULATION OF DELIVERY STATIONS.—(CONTINUED).

C.—THIRD STREET.

	Days open.	General works.	Philosophy.	Theology.	Social and political science.	Philology.	Natural science.	Useful arts.	Fine arts.	Literature.	Prose fiction.	Children's fiction.	History.	Geography.	Biography.	Total circulation.	Date and highest circulation.	Date and lowest circulation.	Daily average.
September, 1889	25	8	3		1		5	1	2	3	70	43	1		2	136	11–10	9– 1	5
October, "	27	9	1				3	1	4	2	82	77		1	1	185	15–14	7– 1	7
November, "	25	16	1	3	2		3		5	5	79	73	3	3	3	196	9–17	11– 2	8
December, "	23	17	1	1	2		3	2	2	3	99	64	2	4	9	209	10–16	16– 4	9
January, 1890	26	16	2		1		1	8	13	4	130	74	11	12	11	283	29–17	23– 5	11
February, "	23	11	1	6	5		10	3	10	27	123	117	35	28	13	389	25–36	7– 6	16
March, "	26	13	2	6	3		10	12	11	13	302	276	13	19	21	696	27–46	24–10	27
April, "	26	22	2	3	1		16	11	10	10	181	339	52	29	6	636	24–42	4–14	24
May, "	26	24	1	9	6		16	8	13	24	178	425	13	33	12	791	6–46	5–11	30
June, "	25	17	3	7	2		29		8	10	144	278	55	43	1	617	7–43	30– 8	25
July, "	26	16	1	1	2		36	3	8	12	95	105	45	21		345	8–24	14– 6	13
August, "	22	11		1	2		34	4	4	12	84	89	34	5	4	285	22–45	28– 3	13
Total	300	180	17	38	27		166	60	90	121	1567	1960	260	198	83	4767	46		115.9
Per cent		3.8	.4	.8	.6		3.5	1.3	1.9	2.5	32.9	41.1	5.4	4.1	1.7				

APPENDIX B.

CIRCULATION OF DELIVERY STATIONS.—(CONTINUED).

D.—WALNUT STREET.

	Days open	General works	Philosophy	Theology	Social and political science	Philology	Natural science	Useful arts	Fine arts	Literature	Prose fiction	Children's fiction	History	Geography	Biography	Total circulation	Date and highest circulation	Date and lowest circulation	Daily average
September, 1889	25			1	2		3	5	2	9	112	53	1	6	2	196	11—10	9—1	5
October, "	27	6	1	3	1			6	4	4	139	80	8	3		249	22—25	4—2	9
November, "	25	10		5			1	5	4	5	124	40	8	7	1	206	13—18	23—3	8
December, "	23			2	1		7		1	10	140	51	13	17	5	256	30—28	31—3	11
January, 1890	26			5	1		10	1	1	8	149	47	11	19	9	255	7—22	6—2	10
February, "	23	2		1	4		11	1		15	119	34	18	22	3	243	25—23	11—1	11
March, "	26	1		1	1		4	8	1	14	187	51	12	10	2	293	18—28	10—3	11
April, "	26	3	3				2	8		18	185	56	13	10	5	298	12—23	7—4	12
May, "	26	3			4		5	6	8	25	172	43	13	10		291	15—23	17—3	11
June, "	25	3	1	1	1		9	2	3	8	170	41	16	11		271	18—19	27—3	11
July, "	26	4	4		4		37	1		14	137	42	24	10		271	24—21	5—6	10
August, "	22			1			31	5	3	12	117	28	18	5	3	231	23—31	14—4	11
Total	300	36	10	22	19		120	48	27	142	1751	566	155	130	34	3060	31	1	12
Per cent		1.2	.3	.7	.6		3.9	1.6	.9	4.6	57.2	18.5	5.1	4.3	1.1				

CIRCULATION OF DELIVERY STATIONS.—(CONTINUED.)

E.—BAY VIEW.

	Days open.	General works.	Philosophy.	Theology.	Social and political science.	Philology.	Natural science.	Useful arts.	Fine arts.	Literature.	Prose fiction.	Children's fiction.	History.	Geography.	Biography.	Total circulation.	Date and highest circulation.	Date and lowest circulation.	Daily average.
September, 1889	25	4			1		1		5	6	69	4	1	3	2	96	14— 7	4— 1	4
October, "	27	1			1			2	12	5	67	25	1	4		118	24— 9	31—1	4
November, "	25	2							9	5	69	14	4	10	4	117	23—11	6—1	5
December, "	23	2		2					8	4	59	13	1	9	11	107	7—11	23—1	5
January, 1890	26	1			1		1	2	5	5	78	14	6	15	5	130	4—10	13—1	5
February, "	23							1	3	3	73	15	5	12	3	119	27—10	4— 2	4
March, "	26			1	2		1		5	5	77	18	6			115	6—11	18—1	4
April, "	26			1			2	4	2	5	66	19	1	5	1	102	4— 8	15—1	4
May, "	25	1			1		1	1		3	80	13	5	5		112	21—13	24-1	3
June, "	26	1					1	1	2	2	67	3	5	3		85	28— 7	9—1	3
July, "	26				1		1		1	2	61	10	1	3		81	23— 9	5—1	3
August, "	22				4		3	2		1	48	11	2			73	22—14	30—1	3
TOTAL	300	12		4	10		11	13	52	43	814	159	38	73	26	1255	14	.	1 4.2
PER CENT.		1.		.3	.8		.9	1	4.1	3.4	64.9	12.7	3.	5.8	2.1				

APPENDIX B.

CIRCULATION OF DELIVERY STATIONS.—(CONTINUED.)

F.—GRAND OPERA HOUSE.

	Days open	General works	Philosophy	Theology	Social and political science	Philology	Natural science	Useful arts	Fine arts	Literature	Prose fiction	Children's fiction	History	Geography	Biography	Total circulation	Date and highest circulation	Date and lowest circulation	Daily average
September, 1889	25		4		9		4		1	20	50	9	12	6	1	116	2—7	13—3	4
October, "	27		6		19		4		1	13	44	5	8	12	3	115	19—7	23—1	4
November, "	25		3		17		3	1	1	33	25	1	11	8	5	107	18—7	27—3	4
December, "	23			8	17				2	28	38	5	9	7	6	113	31—10	23—2	5
January, 1890	26			5	9		1		2	25	25	3	6	2	6	87	25—6	31—2	3
February, "	23			5	4		2	3	4	24	16		3	10	1	72	17—5	26—2	3
March, "	26				1		1		1	10	51		6			72	25—5	24—1	3
April, "	26						2	1			58	1	1	1		76	7—5	29—1	3
May, "	26		1		3		2			8	60	2		1	1	76	28—5	16—1	3
June, "	25				8					5	81		1	2		105	2—7	20—2	4
July, "	26				5		1		1	13	68	2	6	3		95	11—6	10—1	4
August, "	22						8			9	58	3	10			86	22—7	20—2	4
TOTAL	300		14	18	92		28	5	13	1ᵘ2	574	31	76	54	23	1120	10	1	3.7
PER CENT.			1.2	1.6	8.2		2.5	.4	1.2	17.1	51.3	2.8	6.8	4.8	2.1				

APPENDIX B.

CIRCULATION OF DELIVERY STATIONS.—CONTINUED.

G.—SOUTH SIDE, GROVE STREET.

	Days open.	General works.	Philosophy.	Theology.	Social and political science.	Philology.	Natural science.	Useful arts.	Fine arts.	Literature.	Prose fiction.	Children's fiction.	History.	Geography.	Biography.	Total circulation.	Date and highest circulation.	Date and lowest circulation.	Daily average.
September, 1889																			
October, "																			
November, "																			
December, "	23		1	2				2	1	8	42	12		1	1	61	30—16	31—1	3
January, 1890	26	2	2	4	2			4	3	13	87	30	5	12	5	160	2—10	16—1	6
February, "	23			17	1			5	3	7	88	28	11	9	7	184	19—19	17—2	8
March, "	26	2		7	1		3	1	1	5	131	54	10	9	3	228	27—15	10—3	9
April, "	26		2	7	2		1		2	10	134	54	9	14	2	232	24—17	29—3	9
May, "	26	2		7	1		4	1		10	124	75	10	7	5	243	21—17	26—4	9
June, "	25			5	1			4	7	7	82	44	33	2		194	26—15	27—4	8
July, "	26	2		2				2	6	1	61	51	17	6		159	25—13	14—1	6
August, "	22	3		1	7		11	8	2		73	41	19	1	6	173	22—29	29—3	8
TOTAL	223	9	5	52	16		25	27	25	61	822	389	114	60	29	1634	29	1	
PER CENT		.5	.3	3.2	1.		1.5	1.7	1.5	3.7	50.3	23.8	7.	3.7	1.8				7.3

APPENDIX B. (Continued.)

CIRCULATION OF BAY VIEW BRANCH LIBRARY.

	Days open.	General works.	Philosophy.	Theology.	Social and political science.	Philology.	Natural science.	Useful arts.	Fine arts.	Literature.	Prose fiction.	Children's fiction.	History.	Geography.	Biography.	Total circulation.	Date and highest circulation.	Date and lowest circulation.	Daily average.
September, 1889	25				1					9	150	22	4	10	5	201	28—15	26—2	8
October, "	27	1	1							7	126	29	8	8	5	183	12—17	15—1	7
November, "	25		1							13	141	33	5	5	7	203	12—15	7—3	8
December, "	23				1		1	1		15	148	27	7	5	13	222	27—26	20—2	10
January, 1890	26						1			23	153	35	8	7	11	233	2—18	9—3	9
February, "	23									18	145	36	11	12	14	236	21—19	29—5	10
March, "	26	3		1						29	156	43	9	12	14	260	29—16	27—4	10
April, "	26	1	1		1			1		18	140	47	4	10	11	229	14—18	18—1	9
May, "	25			1				1		15	142	27	7	6	11	229	10—18	22—4	9
June, "	26									7	89	29	2	5	3	133	28—10	20—1	5
July, "	26	1								9	99	19	1	4	3	136	10—12	18—2	5
August, "	22									1	93	21	2	4	4	125	20—29	14—1	5
TOTAL	300	6	3	2	3		2	3		164	1582	368	68	88	101	2390	29	18	18.
PER CENT		.2	.1	.1	.1		.1	.1		7.1	66.2	15.4	2.8	3.6	4.2				

APPENDIX B. (Continued.)
CIRCULATION THROUGH SCHOOLS.
1889-90.

	General works	Philosophy	Theology	Social and political science	Philology	Natural science	Useful arts	Fine arts	Literature	Prose fiction	Children's fiction	History	Geography	Biography	Total circulation
September, 1889											82	8			90
October, "	16					55	18	6	51	30	223	70	113	61	643
November, "	23		2	3		44	25	8	43	19	435	102	159	35	879
December, "	119	5	9			127	19	2	49	38	474	60	181	79	1180
January, 1890	23	8	16	12		76	15	13	68	67	596	78	233	69	1262
February, "	22			4		59		31	3	22	158	24	65	19	414
March, "	139			3		122		2	91	85	903	174	383	40	1954
April, "	37		24	5		210	37	19	42	80	436	75	145	60	1174
May, "	365	6	10	13	4	771	121	48	171	266	2519	791	878	214	6173
June, "															
July, "															
August, "															
TOTAL	744	19	61	37	4	1464	244	129	518	607	5826	1382	2157	577	13769
PER CENT.	5.4	.1	.4	.3	.1	10.6	1.8	.9	3.8	4.4	42.3	10.	15.7	4.2	

APPENDIX C.

READING ROOM.

| | DAYS OPEN | | READERS. | | | MAGAZINES. | | | DAILY AVERAGE. | | | |
| | | | | | | | | | READERS. | | MAGAZINES. | |
	Sec. days.	Sun-days.	Secular days.	Sun-days.	Total.	Secular days.	Sun-days.	Total.	Secular days.	Sun-days.	Secular days.	Sun-days.
September, 1889........	24	5	3,989	419	4,408	377	73	450	166	84	16	15
October, "	27	4	5,068	447	5,515	507	70	577	188	112	19	18
November, "	25	4	5,528	465	5,993	561	92	653	221	116	22	23
December, "	23	5	5,955	676	6,531	448	75	523	255	135	19	15
January, 1890........	26	4	6,190	444	6,634	456	65	521	238	111	18	16
February, "	23	4	6,463	546	7,009	433	71	504	281	136	19	18
March, "	26	5	7,356	784	8,140	433	131	564	283	159	17	26
April, "	26	4	6,555	462	7,017	360	48	408	252	116	14	12
May, "	26	4	6,727	379	7,106	331	50	381	259	95	13	13
June, "	25	5	4,653	332	4,985	204	35	239	186	66	8	7
July, "	26	4	4,235	258	4,493	208	25	233	163	65	8	6
August, "	22	4	3,668	411	4,079	265	48	313	167	103	12	12
TOTAL................	299	52	66,287	5,623	71,910	4,583	683	5,266	222	108	15	13

COMPARATIVE SUMMARY OF STATISTICS.

	1878*	1878-7.	1879-80.	1880-1.	1881-2.	1882-3.
Books in Library, beginning of year	9,958	10,024	15,290	16,410	18,649	21,742
Total accessions	66	6,087	1,399	2,447	3,166	2,778
Given	65	149	159	162	833	505
Transferred by binding		88	87	161	146	217
Purchased	1	5,850	1,153	2,124	2,187	2,056
Cost of books actually received	$18.00	$3,834.90	$1,560.52	$3,329.97	$2,640.10	$3,671.53
Worn out and discarded		807	262	109	50	28
Lost, sold and exchanged	1	14	17	13	23	10
Pamphlets, accessions	4	43	-168	326	366	516
Registered book borrowers, beginning of year		1,957	5,350	7,318	10,670	12,888
New names registered	1,957	3,193	1,968	3,351	2,218	2,672
Circulation of books	8,692	91,296	86,328	97,874	88,331	83,052
Working days	48	305½	273	306	305	289
Daily average	181.8	298.8	316.3	319.8	289.8	287.4
Largest issue in one day	327	647	610	697	601	773
Smallest issue in one day	72	132	102	156	101	47
Number of books fined	193	4,680	3,649	4,201	3,439	4,357
Received for fines	$15.53	$394.24	$304.14	$378.13	$303.25	$341.15
Reading room—Magazines on file	28	31	33	70	75	84
Newspapers on file	67	69	64	97	107	107
Visitors				47,467	70,686	66,589
Days open				306	305	289
Average daily attendance				155	232	230
Magazines delivered				6,120	7,646	6,879
Sunday readers		915	4,168	7,141	8,100	8,098
Sundays open		19	48	51	52	50
Average attendance on Sundays		48	87	140	156	162
Magazines delivered				1,063	866	867
Cost of serials	$298.44	$609.12	$438.28	$773.50	$887.33	$887.65
Binding and repairing—number volumes		1,693	1,823	1,000	1,793	892
Cost of binding and repairing		$560.83	$601.45	$443.63	$689.27	$366.63
Appropriation	$8,923.76	$9,330.00	$11,000.00	$11,300.00	$15,567.98	$17,996.87
Amount paid for salaries	$795.35	$3,428.90	$4,075.97	$5,032.28	$5,040.00	$5,351.16

*The statistics for this year comprise only seven weeks from July 8, 1878, when the library was opened to the public.

APPENDIX D.

COMPARATIVE SUMMARY OF STATISTICS—(Continued).

	1883-4.	1884-5.	1885-6.	1886-7.	1887-8.	1888-9.	1889-90.
Books in Library at beginning of year	24,481	28,785	32,499	35,695	42,665	46,357	48,655
Total accessions	4,640	3,842	3,407	7,199	3,920	2,444	4,480
Given	393	759	450	492	557	366	408
Transferred by binding	306	207	22	474	240	436	462
Purchased	3,941	2,876	2,934	5,253	3,123	1,638	3,610
Cost of books actually received	$7,196.67	$5,266.72	$5,067.88	$7,931.48	$5,873.52	$2,372.30	$6,000.71
Worn out and discarded	283	116	170	227	219	136	334
Lost, sold and exchanged	53	12	41	2	9	15	15
Pamphlets, accessions	339	458	256	647	523	587	486
Registered book borrowers, beg. of year	15,560	18,286	20,962	23,760	27,410	31,059	35,840
New names registered	2,726	2,676	2,795	3,650	3,649	4,781	5,437
Circulation of books	87,341	81,399	76,375	97,103	102,754	119,045	144,251
Working days	306	281	279	304	301	300	299
Daily average	285.4	289.7	273.7	319.4	341.3	376.8	482.4
Largest issue in one day	670	645	597	716	666	740	829
Smallest issue in one day	146	132	104	169	173	191	210
Number of books fined	4,760	4,427	3,794	3,812	3,998	4,867	5,474
Received for fines	$381.12	$278.80	$257.18	$234.82	$250.11	$357.94	$409.66
Reading room—Magazines on file	95	98	102	115	144	136	168
Newspapers on file	113	119	117	119	116	74	67
Visitors	73,541	60,205	63,068	70,548	62,465	58,704	66,287
Days open	306	300	300	304	305	300	299
Average daily attendance	240	201	210	232	205	196	222
Magazines delivered	7,892	5,043	4,926	4,560	5,277	4,991	4,583
Sunday readers	8,620	7,719	8,504	8,435	8,152	6,816	5,622
Sundays open	53	51	50	52	49	52	52
Average attendance on Sundays	163	151	170	162	166	131	108
Magazines delivered	914	961	744	742	608	854	683
Cost of serials	$963.49	$1,099.00	$1,149.83	$1,228.96	$1,267.96	$1,026.03	$867.72
Binding and repairing—number volumes	2,020	1,914	1,544	2,339	1,855	2,120	3,155
Cost of binding and repairing	$1,090.45	$967.29	$730.81	$989.89	$905.13	$978.72	$1,338.49
Appropriation	$18,737.93	$19,715.34	$19,715.34	$20,660.44	$22,243.04	$24,137.12	$25,124.55
Amount paid for salaries	$5,792.40	$6,151.21	$6,710.10	$7,097.60	$7,929.32	$7,981.67	$8,340.14

APPENDIX E.

LIST OF GIFTS TO THE LIBRARY.

	Volumes.	Pamphlets.
Ames, W. A., Cambridge, Mass.		3
American federation of labor, New York, N. Y.		1
American institute of architects, New York, N. Y.		2
Amherst, Mass., college		1
Astor library, New York, N. Y.		5
Babcock & Wilcox Co., New York, N. Y.	1	
Barkan, L., Brooklyn, N. Y.	1	
Baltimore, Md., New mercantile library association.		1
Beloit, Wis., college		1
Birmingham, England, free libraries		1
Boston, Mass., Athenæum. Successive bulletins and...		1
" " Ladies' commission on Sunday-school books		1
" " Public library. Successive bulletins...		
Boston & Maine railroad, Boston, Mass.	2	
Boston, Mass., public library		1
Boutell, Lewis H., Chicago, Ill	1	
Bowdoin college, Brunswick, Me.		2
Bradley, Mrs. W. H., Milwaukee, Wis.	1	3
Britt, O. E., Milwaukee, Wis.	1	
Brookline, Mass., public library		1
Brooklyn, N. Y., library		2
Brooklyn, N. Y., Y. M. C. A. library	1	
Brumder, G., Milwaukee, Wis.		2
Brymner, D., Ottawa, Canada	2	
Buck, J. S., Milwaukee	6	
Buffalo, N. Y., library		1
California, state board of trade, San Francisco, Cal..	1	4
California, state library, Sacramento, Cal	1	
California, state mining bureau, Sacramento, Cal	1	1
California university, Berkeley, Cal	1	1
Carpenter, H., Milwaukee		1

U. S., signal bureau	12	3
" state department	1	14
" surgeon-general's office	1	
" war department	10	1
Unknown	3	4
Upsala, Sweden, universitets-biblioteket	3	5
Uxbridge, Mass , free public library		1
Van Schaick, I. W., Washington, D. C	3	
Washington life insurance company, New York, N. Y.	1	
Waterhouse, S., St. Louis, Mo	1	1
Weissert, A. G., Milwaukee	1	
Wellesley, Mass., college		1
Wells, C. K., Milwaukee	19	3
Westinghouse electric company, Pittsburgh, Penn		1
Williams, Norman, Chicago, Ill		1
Wilmington, Del., institute		1
Winchester, Mass., town library		8
Wisconsin, academy of sciences, arts and letters	1	
" state board of health	1	
" state historical society	1	4
" state horticultural society	2	
" state superintendent of public instruction		1
" state superintendent of public property	8	
" university	2	22
Wisconsin central company, Milwaukee		7
Wisconsin Grand lodge, I. O. O. F	1	
Woburn, Mass., public library		1
Woodruff, W., Salt Lake City, Utah	1	
Worcester, Mass., free public library. Successive bulletins and	1	1
Wright, A. G., Milwaukee	1	
Yale university library, New Haven, Conn		5
Yeakle, M. M., St. Louis, Mo	1	
Yewdale, J. H. & Sons Co., Milwaukee	1	
	408	483

APPENDIX F.

NEWSPAPERS AND MAGAZINES ON FILE.

IN THE GENERAL READING ROOM.

AMERICA.

Atlanta, Ga., Southern industrial railroad record, M. (Gift of the publishers.)

Boston, Mass., Advertiser, D.
      Christian register, W. (Gift of the publishers.)
      Civil service record, Irr. (Gift of the publishers.)
      Literary world, SM.
      Office, M.
      Our dumb animals, M. (Gift of the publishers.)
      Popular science news, M.
      Youth's companion, W.

Chicago, Ill., America, W.
      Dial, M.
      Gamla och nya hemlandet, (*Swedish*), W. (Gift of the publishers.)
      Illinois Staatszeitung, (*German*), D.
      Open court, W.
      Skandinaven, (*Norwegian*), D.
      Times, D.
      Tribune, D.
      Union signal, W. (Gift of the publishers.)

Cleveland, O., Silver dollar, SM. (Gift of the publishers.)
Detroit, Mich., Der arme teufel, (*German*), W. (Gift of the publishers.)
Madison, Wis., Northwestern mail, W. (Gift of the publishers.)
      State journal, D.

Medford, Wis., Ansiedler in Wisconsin, (*German*), M.

    Waldbote, (*German*), W.

Milwaukee, Wis., Abend-post (*German*), D.

    Amerikanische turnzeitung, (*German*), W.

    Calumet, W.

    Columbia, (*German*), W.

    Currie's monthly, M.

    Erziehungs-blätter, (*German*), M.

    Evening Wisconsin, D.

    Excelsior, (*German*), W.

    Freidenker, (*German*), W.

    Germania, (*German*), SW.

    Haus-und bauernfreund, (*German*), W.

    Herold, (*German*), D.

    Journal, D.

    Kinder-post, (*German*), W.

    News, D.

    Peck's sun, W.

    Proceedings of the common council, BW.

    Proceedings of the school board, M.

    Saturday star, W.

    Seebote, (*German*), D.

    Sentinel, D.

    Social circle, W.

    Sunday telegraph, W.

    Telephon, (*German*), W.

    United states miller, M.

    Volks-zeitung, (*German*), D.

    Wisconsin times, W.

    Yenowine's Sunday news, W.

    Young churchman, W.

    Zgoda, (*Polish*), W.

New Orleans, La., Picayune, D.

New York, N. Y., Bellestristisches journal, (*German*), W.

    Co-operative index to periodicals, Q.

    Courier des Etats-Unis, (*French*), W.

    Engineering and building record, W.

    Epoch, W.

    Frank Leslie's illustrated newspaper, W.

    Garden and forest, W.

Gift of the publishers.

New York, N. Y., Harpers' weekly, W.

    Iron age, W.

    Judge, W.

    Literary news. M.

    Nation, W.

    Puck, W.

    Staatszeitung, (*German*), D.

    Stockholder, W. (Gift of the publishers.)

    Tribune, D.

    Truth seeker, W. (Gift of the publishers.)

    Voice, W. (Gift of the publishers.)

    Volkszeitung, (*German*), D. (Gift of the publishers.)

    World, D.

Oakland, Cal., American sentinel, W. (Gift of the publishers.)

Omaha, Neb., Bee, D. (Gift of the publishers.)

Philadelphia, Pa., American, W.

San Francisco, Cal., Chronicle, D.

    Californischer volksfreund, (*German*), W. (Gift of the publishers.)

Toronto, Ont., Globe, D.

Washington, D. C., Congressional record, D. (Gift).

    Public opinion, W.

FRANCE.

Paris, L'illustration, W.

GERMANY.

Berlin, Norddeutsche allgemeine zeitung, SD.

Halle, Natur, W.

Leipzig, Gartenlaube, W.

    Illustrirte zeitung, W.

Stuttgart, Ueber land und meer, W.

GREAT BRITAIN AND IRELAND.

Dublin, United Ireland, W.

Glasgow, Herald, W.

London, Academy, W.

    Athenæum, W.

    British journal of photography, W.

    Graphic, W.

    Illustrated news, W.

    Punch, W.

    Saturday review, W.

    Times, W.

Honolulu, Paradise of the pacific M. (Gift of the publishers.)

IN THE LADIES' READING ROOM.

(IN ADDITION TO THOSE IN THE GENERAL ROOM.)

Boston, Mass., Woman's journal, W.
Milwaukee, Wis., Evening Wisconsin, D.
Sentinel, D.
New York, N. Y., Harper's bazar, W.
Harper's weekly, W.
Jenness-Miller magazine, M.

ON APPLICATION AT THE COUNTER IN THE
READING ROOM.

AMERICA.

American antiquarian, Chicago, BM.
American anthropologist, Washington, Q.
American architect and building news, Boston, W.
American chemical journal, Baltimore, BM.
American journal of archæology, Baltimore, Q.
American journal of mathematics, Baltimore, Q.
American journal of philology, Baltimore, Q.
American journal of science, New Haven, M.
American meterological journal, Detroit, M.
American microscopical journal, Washington, M.
American naturalist, Philadelphia, M.
Andover review, Boston, M.
Architectural era, Syracuse, M. (Gift of the publishers.)
Atlantic monthly, Boston, M.
Babyhood, New York, M.
Century magazine, New York, M.
Chautauquan, Meadville, Pa., M.
Cosmopolitan, New York, M.
Church review, New York, M.
Current literature, New York, M.
Eclectic magazine, New York, M.
Electrical engineer, New York, M.
Education, Boston, M.
Etude, Philadelphia, M.

Forum, New York, M.

Harper's monthly, New York, M.

Harper's young people, New York, W.

Journal of american folk-lore, Boston, Q.

Journal of comparative medicine, New York, M.

Journal of morphology, Boston, Irr.

Journal of the Franklin institute, Philadelphia, M.

Keynote, New York, M.

Lippincott's magazine, Philadelphia, M.

Littell's living age, Boston, W.

Magazine of American History, New York, M.

Magazine of western history, New York, M.

New England historical and genealogical register, Boston, Q.

New England magazine, Boston, M.

New review, New York, M.

North American review, New York, M.

Official gazette of the U. S. patent office, Washington, W. (Gift of the
    Patent office.)

Outing, New York, M.

Overland monthly, San Francisco, M.

Political science quarterly, Boston, Q.

Popular science monthly, New York, M.

Quarterly journal of economics, Boston, Q.

Railroad and engineering journal, New York, M.

Queries, Buffalo, M.

St. Nicholas, New York, M.

Sanitarian, New York, M.

Santa Claus, Philadelphia, W.

Science, New York, W.

Scientific American, New York, W.

Scientific American supplement, New York, W.

Scientific American, architects' and builders' edition, New York, M.

Scribner's magazine, New York, M.

Shakespeariana, New York, Q.

Unitarian review, Boston, M. (Gift of the publishers.)

Wide awake, Boston, M.

FRANCE AND ITALY.

Revue des deux mondes, Paris, SM.

Revue internationale, Rome, SM.

GERMANY.

Deutsche revue, Berlin, M.
Deutsche rundschau, Berlin, M.
Geographische mittheilungen, Gotha, M.
Nord und süd, Breslau, M.
Salon, Leipzig, M.
Unsere zeit, Leipzig, M.
Vom fels zum meer, Stuttgart, M.
Westermann's monatshefte, Brunswick, M.

GREAT BRITAIN AND IRELAND.

All the year round, London, W.
Blackwood's Edinburgh magazine, Edinburgh, M.
Chambers's journal, Edinburgh, M.
Contemporary review, London, M.
Cornhill magazine, London, M.
Dublin review, Dublin, Q.
Edinburgh review, Edinburgh, Q.
Engineering, London, W.
English historical review, London, Q.
English illustrated magazine, London, M.
Fortnightly review, London. M.
Geographical society's proceedings, London, M.
Good words, London, M.
London society, London, M.
Longman's magazine, London, M.
Macmillan's magazine, London, M.
Murray's magazine, London, M.
Nature, London, W.
Nineteenth century, London, M.
Observatory, London. M.
Quarterly review, London, Q.
Scottisch review, London, Q.
Temple bar, London, M.
Westminster review, London, M.

IN THE REFERENCE ROOM.

Art amateur, New York, M.
Art journal, London, M.
Magazine of art, London, M.
Portfolio, London, M.

IN THE LIBRARIAN'S ROOM.

Allgemeine bibliographie für Deutschland, Leipzig, W.

American notes and queries, Philadelphia, W.

Antiquary, London, M.

Appleton's literary bulletin, New York, M.   (Gift of the publishers.)

Author, Boston, M.

Book buyer, New York, M.

Book chat, New York, M.

Bookmart, Pittsburgh, M.

Book prices current, London, M.

Book worm, London, M.

Catalogue mensuel de la librairie française, Paris, M.

Centralblatt für bibliothekswesen, Leipzig, M.

Critic, New York, W.

Deutsche literaturzeitung, Berlin, W.

Hinrichs' Bücherverzeichniss, Leipzig, Q. and SA.

Index of current events, Montreal, M.

Insect life, Washington, M.   (Gift of the department of agriculture.)

Johns Hopkins university circulars, Baltimore, M.   (Gift of the pubs.)

Library, London, M.

Library journal, New York, M.

Literary news, New York, M.

Literary world, Boston, SM.

Literarischer merkur, Leipzig, SM.

Livre moderne, Le, Paris, M.

Notes and queries, London, W.

Publishers' circular, London, SM.

Publishers' weekly, N. Y., W.

Torch and colonial book circular, London, Q.

U. S. government publications monthly catalogue, Wash., M.

Writer, Boston, M.

Zeitschrift für vergleichende literaturgeschichte, Berlin, BM.

Explanation of abbreviations used to denote frequency of publication: SD—twice a day; D—daily; W—weekly; SW—twice a week; BW—every two weeks; SM—twice a month; M—monthly; BM—every two months; Q—four times a year; SA—twice a year.

ACTS OF THE WISCONSIN LEGISLATURE RELATING TO THE PUBLIC LIBRARY.

LAWS OF 1878—CHAPTER 6.

AN ACT relating to the Young Men's Association of the city of Milwaukee, and amendatory of chapter 97 of the laws of 1852.

The people of the State of Wisconsin, represented in senate and assembly, do enact as follows:

SECTION 1. The board of directors of the Young Men's Association of the city of Milwaukee are hereby authorized and empowered, in the name and behalf of said association, to assign, transfer and convey to the city of Milwaukee, all and singular, the books, cabinets, library, furniture, apparatus, fixtures and other property of whatsoever nature, belonging to said association, in trust, to be kept, supported and maintained by said city as a free public library, for the benefit and use of all the citizens of said city, *provided*, the said city shall accept the trust and assume the care and maintenance of such library.

SEC. 2. Before making such transfer and conveyance, the said board of directors shall pay, or provide for paying, all the known debts and liabilities of said association, and with and upon the completed conveyance, transfer and delivery of said property by said board, and its acceptance and assumption by said city, the said Young Men's Association shall be deemed to be dissolved, and its franchise, as a corporation, to be surrendered to the state; *provided*, the power of the present board of directors shall be continued six months from the date of the passage of this act, for the sole purpose of winding up the affairs and settling the concerns of said association.

SEC. 3. This act shall take effect and be in force from and after its passage.

Approved February 7, 1878.

LAWS OF 1878—CHAPTER 7.

AN ACT to establish and maintain a public library in the city of Milwaukee, (*as amended*).

The people of the State of Wisconsin, represented in senate and assembly, do enact as follows:

SECTION 1. The city of Milwaukee is hereby authorized to establish and maintain a public library therein, for the free use of the inhabitants thereof, and to receive, hold and manage any devise, bequest or donation for the establishment, increase and maintenance of such library under such regulations as are herein contained, or as may hereafter be adopted, as provided in this act.

SEC. 2. The public library, established under this act, shall be considered a branch of the educational department of the city of Milwaukee, and shall be under the general management, control and supervision of a board, consisting of nine members, who shall be styled, "The Board of Trustees of the Public Library of the city of Milwaukee."

SEC. 3. The president of the school board, and the superintendent of public schools of said city, shall be ex-officio members of said board of trustees. William Frankfurth, Gustave C. Trumpff, Matthew Keenan and John

Johnston, residents and taxpayers of the city of Milwaukee, and three members of the common council of said city, to be appointed as hereinafter provided, together with said president of the school board, and said superintendent of public schools, shall be, and are hereby constituted, the first board of trustees. The four trustees above designated by name shall serve for one, two, three and four years from the date of organization of said board, so that the term of one of them shall expire each year. The respective terms of these four trustees shall be determined by lot at the first meeting of said board after the passage of this act, and their places shall be filled, whenever a vacancy shall occur, by election by the board, from among the citizens at large, and annually, upon the expiration of the term of any such designated trustee, the board shall, at their annual meeting, elect from among the citizens and tax payers of said city, his successor, to serve for the term of four years. [The first three members from the common council shall be appointed by the mayor of said city, at the first meeting of the council held for organization after the charter election in 1878, from the members of the common council, to-wit: one from the three year class of aldermen, one from the two year class of aldermen, and one from the one year class of aldermen, who shall serve as such trustees during their respective terms as such aldermen. And annually, on the third Tuesday in April thereafter, at the expiration of the term of any such trustee, the mayor shall appoint his successor for the term of three years, from the aldermen then having three years to serve. In case any person so appointed trustee shall vacate the office of alderman before the expiration of his term, he shall at the same time cease to be a member of said board of trustees, and the mayor shall appoint some other alderman of his class in his place for the balance of his term.*] None of the said trustees shall receive any compensation from the city treasurer, or otherwise, for their services as such trustees. And no member of said board of trustees shall become, or cause himself to become interested, directly or indirectly, in any contract or job for the purchase of books, pamphlets or other matter pertaining to the library, or of fuel, furniture, stationery or things necessary for the increase and maintenance of the library.

SEC. 4. The first annual meeting of the board of trustees shall be held on the sixth day of May, 1878, at which meeting the board shall organize, by the choice of one of their number as president, to serve for one year, and until his successor shall have been chosen. And it shall be the duty of the city clerk of said city, as soon as practicable after the appointment of the three trustees to be selected from the common council, to give at least three days' notice, in writing, of such meeting of organization, to be held at the office of said city clerk on the said sixth day of May, 1878, to every member of said board. And all subsequent annual meetings of said board shall be held on the second Monday of May in each year, at which a president shall be chosen from their number, to serve for one year, and until his successor shall be chosen.

SEC. 5. The board of trustees shall have general care, control and supervision of the public library, its appurtenances, fixtures and furniture, and of the selection and purchase of books, pamphlets, maps, and other matters appertaining to a public library; and also of the disbursement of all moneys appropriated for and belonging to the library fund, in the manner hereinafter provided. And said board shall adopt, and at their discretion modify, amend or repeal by-laws, rules and regulations for the

---

*See amendment, Laws of 1887, page 53 of this report.

management, care and use of the public library, and fix
and enforce penalties for their violation, and generally
shall adopt such measures as shall promote the public
utility of the library; *provided*, that such by-laws, rules,
and regulations shall not conflict with the provisions of
this act.

SEC. 6 (*As amended by chapter* 152, *laws of* 1879).
The board of trustees shall, at their first meeting, on the
sixth day of May, 1878, or thereafter, as soon as practicable, and every five years thereafter, at an annual meet.
ing, elect by ballot a person of suitable learning, ability
and experience for librarian, who shall also act and be ex-
officio secretary of said board of trustees, who shall hold
his office for five years from the time of said first annual
meeting, unless previously removed, and who shall receive
such compensation as may be hereafter fixed by the said
board of trustees. And said board of trustees shall also
appoint such assistants and employés for said library as
they may deem necessary and expedient, and shall fix
their compensation. All vacancies in the office of librarian, assistants or other employés, shall be filled by said
board of trustees, and the person so selected or appointed
shall hold for the unexpired term.

SEC. 7. The librarian elected under this act may be
removed from office for misdemeanor, incompetency or
inattention to the duties of his office, by a vote of two-
thirds of the board of trustees; the assistants and other
employés may be removed by the board for incompetency,
or for any other cause.

SEC. 8. (*As amended by chapter* 152, *laws of* 1879).
It shall be the duty of the board of trustees, within ten
days after the appointment of the librarian and other
salaried employés, to report and file with the city comp-

troller, a duly certified list of the persons so appointed, with the salary allowed to each, and the time or times fixed for the payment thereof, and they shall also furnish such comptroller with a list of all accounts and bills which may be allowed by said board of trustees, stating the character of the materials or service for which the same were rendered, immediately after the meeting of said board, at which such allowance shall be made. And said board of trustees shall also, on or before the first day of October in each year, make to the common council a report, made up to and including the 31st day of August of the said year, containing a statement of the condition of the library, the number of books added thereto, the number of books circulated, and the number of books not returned or lost, together with such information or suggestions as they may deem important; and this report shall contain an account of the moneys credited to the library fund, and expended on account of the same during the preceding year.

SEC. 9. (*As amended by chapter* 152, *laws of* 1879, and *chapter* 60, *laws of* 1882). The common council shall levy and collect annually upon all taxable property in said city, at the same time and in the same manner as other city taxes are levied and collected by law, a special tax of one-fourth of a mill upon each dollar of the assessed value of said taxable property, and the entire amount of said special tax shall be paid into and held in the city treasury as a separate and distinct fund, to be known as the "library fund," and the same shall not be used or appropriated, directly or indirectly, for any other purpose than for the maintenance and increase of the public library, the payment of the salaries of the librarian, assistants and other employés of the library, the purchase of books, furniture, supplies and fuel, the expenses of rent and insurance, and the incidental expenses, including incidental repairs of the library rooms and furniture.

SEC. 10. (*As amended by chapter* 152, *laws of* 1879.) The board of trustees shall erect, purchase, hire or lease buildings, lots, rooms and furniture for the use and accommodation of said public library, and shall improve, enlarge and repair such library buildings, rooms and furniture; but no lot or building shall be purchased, or erected, or enlarged for the purpose herein mentioned, without an ordinance or resolution of the common council of said city, and deeds of conveyance and leases shall run to the city of Milwaukee.

SEC. 11. All moneys received by, or raised in, the city of Milwaukee for library purposes shall be paid over to the city treasurer, to be disbursed by him on the orders of the president and secretary of the board of trustees, countersigned by the city comptroller. Such order shall be made payable to the order of the persons in whose favor they shall have been issued, and shall be the only vouchers of the city treasurer for the payments from the library fund. The said board of trustees shall provide for the purchase of books, supplies, fuel and other matters necessary for the maintenance of the library; *provided, however,* that it shall not be lawful for said board of trustees to expend or contract a liability for any sum in excess of the amount levied in any one year for the library fund on account of such fund.

SEC. 12. In case the Young Men's Association of the city of Milwaukee shall donate or transfer to the city of Milwaukee its library, fixtures, furniture and other property for the purposes of a free public library, it shall be lawful for said city to accept such donation and transfer, and the board of trustees herein created shall assume the charge and control of said property. It shall also be lawful for said city to receive money, books and other property by devise, bequest or gift from any person or corporation, for library purposes, and to employ or invest the same for the use and benefit of the public library, so far as practicable, in conformity with the conditions and terms of such device, bequest or gift.

SEC. 13 In case said Young Men's Association shall make the transfer and donation mentioned in the preceding section, and said city shall accept the same before the date of the annual meeting in May, 1878, as provided in this act, then immediately upon such transfer and acceptance it shall be the duty of the mayor to appoint three aldermen, who, together with the trustees hereinbefore designated by name, and the president of the school board of said city, and the superintendent of public schools, shall constitute a temporary board of trustees, who, until the time of such annual meeting, shall be clothed with all the powers and responsibilities hereinbefore provided, and shall assume the charge, control and management of the property thus donated and accepted, and shall hold and manage the same as provided in this act.

Sec. 14. This act shall take effect and be in force from and after its passage and publication.

Approved February 7, 1878.

LAWS OF 1879—CHAPTER 152

AN ACT to amend an act entitled an act to establish and maintain a public library in the city of Milwaukee, approved February 7, 1878.

The people of the state of Wisconsin, represented in senate and assembly, do enact as follows:

Sec.4. All moneys, books and other property received by the city of Milwaukee by devise, bequest or gift from any person or corporation, for library purposes, shall, unless otherwise directed by the donors, be under the management and control of said board of trustees; and all moneys derived from fines and penalities for violations of the rules of the library, or from any other source, in the course of the administration of the library, including all moneys which may be paid to the city upon any policy or policies of insurance or other obligation of liability for or on account of loss or damage to any property pertaining to the library, shall belong to the "library fund" in the city treasury, to be disbursed on the orders of said board of trustees, countersigned by the city comptroller, for library purposes, in addition to the amount levied and raised by taxation for such fund.

Sec. 6. This act shall take effect and be in force from and after its passage and publication.

Approved March 1, 1879.

LAWS OF 1887—CHAPTER 521.

AN ACT to amend......chapter 7, of the laws of 1878, to establish a public library in the city of Milwaukee.

The people of the state of Wisconsin, represented in senate and assembly, do enact as follows:

Sec. 1 Hereafter all appointments of members from the common council of the board of trustees of the public library of the city of Milwaukee, made by the mayor on the third Tuesday in April, shall be made from aldermen having two years to serve, and in case any person so appointed shall

54

vacate his office of alderman before the expiration of his term, he shall thereupon cease to be a member of said board of trustees, and the mayor shall appoint some other alderman of his class in his place, to be such trustee for the remainder of his term. Each alderman appointed shall serve as such trustee during his term as alderman. It shall be the duty of the mayor, on the third Tuesday in April in each year, to appoint a sufficient number of aldermen having two years to serve as aldermen, to be members of such board of trustees, to keep the number of members of such board from the common council always three. All provisions of chapter 7 of the laws of 1878 which in any way conflict with the foregoing provisions of this section are hereby amended accordingly.

Approved April 14, 1887.

BY-LAWS OF THE BOARD OF TRUSTEES.

8. Election of officers.

9. New business.

ART. 5. The records of the proceedings of the board of trustees and its commitees shall be kept in the secretary's office, and shall be open at all times to inspection and examination by any member of the board.

ART. 6. The by-laws and rules of the board may be temporarily suspended by unanimous consent of all members present; but no permanent alteration or amendment shall be acted upon until the next regular meeting after the same shall have been proposed, unless each member of the board has been supplied with written copies of the proposed changes at least one week before the meeting of the board.

ART. 7. The rules of parliamentary practice comprised in Robert's Rules of Order shall govern the proceedings of the board in all cases to which they are applicable, and in which they do not conflict with these by-laws, rules and regulations.

OFFICERS.

ART. 8. At the annual meeting in May the board shall elect by ballot a president, whose duty it shall be to preside at all meetings of the board,—to sign all warrants drawn on the city treasurer by order of the board,—to appoint the standing commitees for the year,—to prepare, for the consideration and approval of the board, the annual report of the board of trustees, required by the eighth section of the Public Library act,—and otherwise perform all duties incident to his office.

ART. 9. In the temporary absence or other inability of the president to perform his duties, the board shall elect one of their number president pro tempore.

ART. 10. The duties of the librarian, elected under the provisions of the sixth article of the Public Library act

shall be as follows:—to take charge of the library and
reading room, and he shall be responsible for the care and
safety of the books and other public property contained
therein; —to submit to the board of trustees, and to the
proper committees, measures for securing the proper management and fullest efficiency of the library and reading
room; —to obtain for the library public documents of all
kinds, as well as the publications of libraries, library
associations, and other bodies, whose proceedings and
reports may afford information of value to the board or
the users of the library;—to keep carefully arranged, for
the use of the board, lists of new books and publications,
both American and foreign;—to prepare for the use of the
board list of books and periodicals required to complete
sets, to fill out such departments as are deficient, and to
supply the place of books which have been lost;—to keep
a list of all books or publications donated to the library,
stating the name and residence of the donor and the date
when received;—to classify and arrange all books and
publications as soon as received, and to keep the same
catalogued according to such plan or plans as may be
approved by the board;—to report promptly all flagrant
cases of theft, mutilation or injury of books and periodicals;—to be responsible for the preservation of order in
the rooms, and to be present, so far as library business
will permit, in the library during library hours, except
during the evening;—to exercise control over the library
and reading room, and all employés of the board, and to
promptly report to the executive committee any delinquency on the part of the employés;—to keep exact and
detailed accounts of all moneys received from fines and
other sources, and report the same monthly to the board
at the regular meeting;—to submit monthly a report of
all books added to and loaned by the library;—to prepare

and submit to the board an annual report, giving a full
account of the working of the library during the year
ending and including August 31st, said report to accompany the annual report of the board to the common
council;—to discharge such other duties as fall within the
province of librarian, and may from time to time be prescribed by the board;—but in the performance of his duties
as above specified, no debt or liability of any kind shall
be incurred by him without express authority from the
board.

Art. 11. It shall be the duty of the librarian, as secretary of the board of trustees, to be present at all meetings
of the board and of the committees, and to keep full and
correct reports of their proceedings;—to keep books of
account in which all the money transactions of the board
shall be set forth accurately in detail and to make out
and sign all warrants drawn on the city treasurer by order
of the board;—to take care of all business papers of the
board, and to keep the same neatly filed for convenient
reference;—to prepare and submit in his monthly report a
statement of the finances of the library;—to give notice of
all meetings of the board, and of committees, at least
twenty-four hours before the time of meeting;—to transact
all such other business as may be required of him by the
board and its committees.

Art. 12. The librarian shall be required to give bonds
with two or more sureties, in the sum of $3,000, for the
faithful performance of his duties, to be approved by the
board and filed with the city comptroller.

Art. 13. For all fines, security deposits and other payments to the library, the librarian shall give his receipt in
such form as to show the amount received in duplicate,
one part to be given to the payer and the other kept at
.the library for permanent reference,—and no claim for

undue charges shall be considered by the board, unless the proper receipt shall be submitted in evidence.

ART. 14. All funds received from time to time as fines for overdue books, through sales of catalogues or bulletins, and from all other sources, except security deposits for the safe return of library property, shall be paid by the librarian into the treasury, for the credit of the library fund, at the end of each quarter of the fiscal year of the library.

ART. 15. The board shall elect, from among the regular employés of the library, a suitable person as deputy librarian, who shall exercise the powers and perform the duties of the librarian in his absense or other inability.

ART. 16. In case of a vacancy in the office of president, secretary, or the elected members of the board, such vacancy shall be filled by an election at any regular meeting, or at a special meeting called for that purpose.

COMMITTEES.

ART. 17. The standing committees of the board shall be, (1) the executive committee, (2) the committee on library and reading room, (3) the committee on finance and auditing, (4) the committee on library service. Each of these committees, with the exception of the committee on library service, shall consist of three members, the president being, ex-officio, a member of the executive committee.

ART. 18. The executive committee shall have supervision of all matters relating to the construction, leasing, repairing and furnishing of the rooms or building occupied by the library,—of insuring its property,—and of the order and cleanliness of its rooms.

ART. 19. The committee on library and reading rooms shall have supervision of all matters relating to the selection, purchase and binding of books, periodicals and pamphlets,—the exchange or sale of duplicate or other books,—

the arrangement and classification of books,—their preparation for use,—their use and circulation,—their withdrawal from circulation,—the acceptance or rejection of donations,—and the preparation, printing and distribution or sale of catalogues; *provided*, that in all such matters no action shall be taken by the committee until approved by the board. All questions relating to the regulations governing the use of the library, and any proposed addition or amendment thereto, shall be referred to this committee before action is taken by the board.

ART. 20. The committee on finance and auditing shall have supervision of all matters relating to the accounts and account books of the library. It shall be their duty to prepare the annual budget of the board,—to direct the manner of keeping and to examine the account books of the library,—to examine the monthly and other financial statement of the librarian and secretary, and certify to the correctness of the same,—to examine and audit all vouchers and accounts against the library,—and make such suggestions, from time to time, concerning the finances of the library, as they may deem advisable.

ART. 21. A majority of any committee shall constitute a quorum, for the transaction of business under its supervision or referred to it.

ART. 22. It shall be the duty of the several committees to hold monthly meetings, for the purpose of acting upon the matters belonging or referred to them respectively, at such times as each committee may determine for itself, and due notice of every such meeting shall be given to the members of the committee by the secretary. A special meeting of a committee may be called by any member thereof, and at least twenty-four hours' previous notice shall be given, in writing, to the members of the committee by the secretary, stating the object of such meeting.

ART. 23. All reports shall be written and signed by the proper committee. All resolutions shall be in writing, and, if required by any member, motions shall be reduced to writing before being acted upon by the board.

LIBRARY SERVICE.

ART. 24. All applications for permanent positions as assistants in the public library shall be referred to a committee, to be called the committee on library service, and to consist of four members of the board and the librarian. This committee, in determining the fitness of candidates for employment by the board, and in recommending appointments, shall be governed by the following rules:

ART. 25. Every application for regular appointment in the public library, together with recommendations if any, relating to such application, shall be kept on file by the secretary in a separate envelope, and in such form as shall exhibit to members of the board the full name, address, age, place of birth, education, and present or past occupation of the applicant.

ART. 26. It shall be the duty of the librarian, under direction of the committee, to examine, at such time and place as shall be publicly announced in the local press, candidates making application as required in the preceding article. Questions for this examitation shall be submitted for the approval of the committee on library service, or of any of its members that shall be selected by said committee.

ART. 27. The examination of all candidates shall be conducted in writing, and shall include such questions as shall test the general knowledge of the applicants, their ability to use the English language correctly in conversation and composition, and their knowledge of such branches as are deemed especially useful to persons employed as assistants in the public library.

ART. 28. All examination papers written by applicants shall be designated by a number, and be accompanied by a sealed envelope bearing the same number and containing the full name and address of the writer, and all papers bearing the name of their writers shall be rejected.

ART. 29. The librarian shall examine the papers submitted by applicants and mark the same upon a uniform basis and upon a scale of one hundred. He shall present these papers, with the record of standing and the sealed envelopes containing the key to their authors, to the committee on library service.

ART. 30. The committee on library service shall open the envelopes and report to the board the result of the examination, and shall further report on the personal qualifications of candidates, their moral character, behavior and bearing, with any other fact, commendatory or otherwise. But, in determining the preference of candidates, no facts connected with the necessities of the applicants, their relationships, religion, politics, or social position, shall be reported by the committee or considered by the board.

ART. 31. All papers, written reports and records of standing of applicants shall be kept on file by the librarian, and shall be open for inspection by responsible persons; but no papers or other documents connected with the examinations shall be taken from the custody of the librarian.

ART. 32. The library board, upon receiving the report of the committee on library service, shall proceed to elect persons to fill vacancies from those candidates having the highest standing in scholarship, as shown by examination, and whose moral character and personal bearing is favorably reported upon by the committee.

ART. 33. All appointments to fill vacancies in the library shall be on three months' trial, after which, upon favorable report by the librarian and action by the board, employés shall be deemed permanently appointed.

RULES GOVERNING EMPLOYES.

ARTICLE 1. The term of service of the deputy librarian and employés of the public library shall be during good behavior, and they shall only be removed for cause, of which the board shall be the exclusive judge.

ART. 2. The librarian and deputy librarian, and all regular employés, not specially detailed for evening service, shall report daily for duty at 8:30 A. M., except on Sundays and legal holidays. An open record of the times of arrival and departure of all employés shall be kept for the inspection of the members of the board, and it shall be the duty of all employés to report daily to the librarian, or such person as he may designate, the exact time in the forenoon, afternoon or evening, at which they begin and cease service.

ART. 3. The length of a day's service shall be eight hours, and the duties of regular employés shall be arranged by the librarian so as to allow, as nearly as possible, equal leisure for meals and to assign to each an equitable portion of evening work or special service.

ART. 4. The librarian shall report to the board at the regular monthly meeting all written complaints against attendants, charging them with discourtesy or inattention to duty. He shall further report to what extent the time of each and everyé employ is occupied, the number of days' or hours' absence of each employé, and the cause of absence,—the number of times tardy, and the time lost by tardiness,—and any and all facts regarding the efficiency of persons employed in the library; said report to include also a statement of the absences of the librarian and the deputy librarian.

Art. 5. In cases of absence, other than absence upon the annual vacation granted by the board, the monthly salary of employés shall be diminished in the ratio which the length of absence bears to the number of working days in the month, reckoning eight hours for one day's service; except in cases of absence caused by sickness or death in the family of employés, in which case the deduction shall be one-half the regular salary, determined in the ratio above mentioned.

Art. 6. In making deduction for absences, the salaries of employés who have been absent during any month or part of a month, shall be audited by the finance committee with the librarian, and the action of said committee shall be reported to the board at its next meeting.

Art. 7. All employés of the library shall be subject to suspension by the librarian, for absenting themselves without leave, want of attention to business, unreasonable waste of time, discourtesy to users of the library, or improper behavior generally. Whenever an employé of the library is suspended, the librarian shall immediately report the same to the executive committee, and shall submit to the board at its next regular meeting, a full statement of the matter.

Art. 8. In case of the absence of an employé, where service is urgently needed, the librarian shall have power to employ a suitable person as substitute, at a compensation to be fixed by the executive committee, and report his action to the board, at the next meeting, for consideration and approval.

Art. 9. In the absence of the librarian, the deputy librarian shall assume full management of all matters appertaining to the library and the duties or service of employés.

ART. 10. A copy of these rules for the goverment of employés in the library shall be printed and hung in such place in the reading room, reference department and issuing department, as shall be convenient for perusal by the public and by employés.

RULES GOVERNING DELIVERY STATIONS.

ART. 1. For the benefit of residents of the city living at a distance from the library, the board shall maintain three or more distributing stations for the delivery of books to persons who are entitled to the privileges of the library, and have complied with the requirements made and provided for the drawing of books. The stations shall be located by the committee on library and reading room, subject to approval by the board. They shall be situated as far as practicable, at such points as will accommodate the largest number of residents living in parts of the city from which the library is not conveniently accessible. They shall be selected with a view to agreeableness and quietness of surroundings, and admit of being freely visited by adults and youth of both sexes.

ART. 2. The person in charge of the premises where books are distributed, shall receive a compensation for the care of library property and for services performed, the amount of such compensation to be determined by the library committee and approved by the board. Such person or persons shall sign the following agreement, which shall be submitted to and accepted by the board in each case, viz:

I, ..., hereby agree to perform the duties of distributing agent for the board of trustees of the Mil-

waukee Public Library for the period of.....................from
the date hereof, in accordance with the rules prescribed by
said board; and for all services performed as such agent, I
hereby agree to accept the sum total of $...... per month,
which amount shall include all claims made by me against
said library board for rent of room or space in which to
deposit library property, and books awaiting delivery or
return to the library.

ART. 3. Distributing agents shall deliver books to cardholders, and receive books, cards and lists in application
for books, between 9 A. M. and 8 P. M. of all days during
which their places of business are open to the public.

They shall wait upon book borrowers with as much
promptness as circumstances will permit,—keep in sight
and convenient for public use such catalogues and notices
as the library board shall supply for the purpose,—exercise
vigilance in the care of property belonging to the library,
and see that book borrowers are courteously treated and
accommodated in all reasonable requests for books and
information respecting the use of the library.

ART. 4. Distributing agents shall obey fully and
promptly any request of the librarian in regard to the retention or return to the library of any and all books or
property, and shall make such reports as to the condition
or number of books on hand, or as to the condition of any
library property, and shall give such information concerning the same as the librarian may request.

ART. 5. It shall be the duty of the distributing agent to
receive books delivered from the library,—to place and
secure the same in repositories provided for the purpose by
the library board,—to pack ready for immediate transfer
to the library at the call of the carrier all books and cards
left at the station by borrowers,—to notify the librarian
immediately of any loss of property belonging to the

library or damage to the same,—and generally to assist in promoting the interest of the public and the usefulness of the library.

ART. 6. The committee on library and reading room shall engage a responsible person, acceptable to the board, and at a compensation approved by the board, to transfer books and other property between the library and the distributing stations. The frequency of delivery of book packages shall be regulated by special act of the board, but not less than one delivery a day shall be made for a period of six months from adoption of these rules.

ART. 7. The committee on library shall have general charge of the delivery station system and shall report to the board at the regular monthly meeting all matters of importance relating thereto, and make such recommendations as they deem necessary to sustain and increase the efficiency of this department of the library service.

ART. 8. The librarian shall keep a separate account of each delivery station, specifying the number and classes of all books distributed through each agency, as required in Art. 5 of these rules, and at the regular monthly meeting of the board, and in his annual report, he shall enter separately and distinctly the statistics of the distribution of each station, with such other facts as he may deem of interest to the public and of importance to the board.

ART. 9. These rules shall be printed, and a copy furnished each of the station keepers, for posting in a conspicuous place.

REGULATIONS.

ARTICLE 1. The library shall be open on all secular days from 9 o'clock A. M. to half-past 8 o'clock P. M. The reading rooms shall be open from the same hour to 9 o'clock P. M.

ART. 2. Any person of good deportment and habits may use the reading room. The use of tobacco, and all conversation, and other conduct not consistent with the quiet and orderly use of the reading room, are prohibited.

ART. 3. Any resident of Milwaukee may draw books from the library by signing an agreement to observe all the rules and regulations of the library and complying with either of the following conditions:

1. Giving satisfactory security in the form following:

Milwaukee,..................................18...

I, the subscriber, hereby certify that.............. ....
residing at No...............................Street, is a fit person to
enjoy the privileges of the Milwaukee Public Library, and
for value received, I agree that I will be responsible for
the observance by............of the regulations of the library,
and will make good any injury or loss the library may
sustain from or by reason of the permission to draw
books that may be given in consequence of this certificate.

(Signed)...
Residing at No.................Street.

"N. B. — The privileges granted in consequence of this certificate shall terminate at the end of two years from its date and may be sooner revoked, at pleasure, by the librarian or board of trustees of the library, or by the signer."

2. Depositing three dollars, and, in special cases, such further sum as the value of the book asked for may, in the judgment of the librarian, require. For such deposits receipts shall be given.

ART. 4. Each person entitled to draw books from the library will be supplied with a card, inscribed with his or her name, residence and register number. This card must be produced whenever a book is taken, returned or renewed. *Immediate notice of a change of residence must be given at the library.* Neglect to give this notice will subject the card-holder to forfeiture of privileges.

ART. 5. The holder of a card is entitled to draw one volume if octavo or larger size; or two volumes of smaller size than octavo, they being the same work.

ART. 6. Books may be retained two weeks, and may be once renewed for the same period. Application for renewal must be made within the first fourteen days.

ART. 7. Books of recent purchase, labeled "Seven Day Book," cannot be retained more than one week and cannot be renewed.

ART. 8. Encyclopedias, dictionaries and other works of reference, elaborately illustrated books, and such others as may be unsuited for general circulation, can be used only in the reference room.

ART. 9. A fine of three cents a day shall be paid on each volume which is not returned according to the provisions of the preceding rules; and no book will be delivered to the party incurring the fine till it is paid.

ART. 10. Writing in books is prohibited; and all injuries to books, beyond reasonable wear, and all losses, shall be promptly adjusted to the satisfaction of the librarian.

ART. 11. Delinquents will be notified through the mail, on the third day after their delinquency has occurred; and one week thereafter, if the book is not returned, the guarantor will be notified. If the book is not returned within twenty days after serving the first notice, the librarian shall proceed to collect, through the law department of the city, the value of the book, with accrued fines and other charges to the date of payment.

ART. 12. Any person abusing the privileges of the library, or violating these regulations, shall be temporarily suspended from the use of the library, and the case shall be reported to the library committee for proper action thereon.

ART. 13. The library cards of persons by whom fines or charges have been or shall be incurred, and who shall neglect to pay such fines or charges within thirty days after they were incurred, shall be cancelled by the librarian; and no card shall be issued to any such delinquent until all such fines and charges shall have been paid.

ART. 14. The written certificate or guaranty, furnished under Art. 3, shall only entitle the person for whom it is given, to the privileges of the library for two years from its date, or until sooner revoked by the librarian, the board of trustees of the library, or by the signer of such certificate. And upon the expiration of such two years, or upon such revocation, the card of the book-borrower shall be surrendered and canceled, and no further book shall be delivered to him or her, until new and satisfactory security shall be given under said Art. 3.

ART. 15. In case of the loss of a barrower's card, immediate notice thereof must be given to the librarian, and, upon application, a duplicate card may be issued to the borrower, upon the payment of a fine of ten cents.

ART. 16. The drawing of books through the various distributing stations, established by the board of trustees shall be governed by the same regulations as prescribed for the use of the general library. Blanks for the agreement and guaranty stipulated in Art. 3 will be furnished by the agent at each station, who will transmit them, when properly filled out, to the librarian. Fines imposed for delinquencies may be paid to the agent for transmission to the library, at the same time that the book is returned, or at any other time, but any error made by the agent in the calculation of fines will be corrected by the librarian, and must be settled before another book is issued.

GENERAL LAW OF THE STATE OF WISCONSIN FOR THE PROTECTION OF PUBLIC LIBRARIES.

LAWS OF 1875—CHAPTER 270.

AN ACT to protect public libraries, and the libraries of literary, scientific, historical and library associations and societies.

The people of the State of Wisconsin, represented in senate and assembly, do enact as follows:

Section 1. Any person who shall willfully, maliciously or wantonly, tear, deface, mutilate, or by other means injure any book, pamphlet, map, chart, painting or picture belonging to any public library, or to any library, the property of any literary, scientific, historical or library society or association, whether incorporated or unincorporated, shall be deemed guilty of a misdeanor, and, on conviction thereof shall be punished by a fine of not less than five dollars, nor more than one hundred dollars, or by imprisonment in the county jail of not less than ten nor more than sixty days, in the discretion of the court; and all justices of the peace in their respective counties shall have jurisdiction to hear, try and determine all prosecutions under this act.

Sec. 2. Any person who shall procure or take, in any way whatever, from the library of any public library, or library of any literary, scientific, historical or library society or association whatever, incorporated or not, any book, pamphlet, map, chart, painting or picture, with intent to convert the same to his own use, or who shall convert the same to his own use with intent to defraud the owner thereof, shall be punished by a fine of not less than ten nor more than one hundred dollars, or, in the discretion of the court, by imprisonment in the county jail for not more than three months.

SEC. 3. It shall be the duty of every librarian, board of trustees, directors or other officers or persons having charge or control of any such library as is mentioned in this act, to post up, in one or more conspicuous place in the room or rooms where the same shall be kept, a printed copy of this act.

SEC. 4. This act shall take effect and be in force from and after its passage and publication.

Approved March 5, 1875.

CONTENTS.

FOURTEENTH AND FIFTEENTH · ·

ANNUAL REPORTS

OF THE · · · · · ·

BOARD OF TRUSTEES

OF THE · · · · · · · ·

PUBLIC ▲

LIBRARY

OF THE · · · · · ·

CITY OF MILWAUKEE.

OCTOBER 1ST, 1892.

STANDARD PRINTING COMPANY, 114 MICHIGAN STREET,
MILWAUKEE.

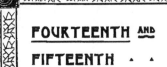

FOURTEENTH & FIFTEENTH

ANNUAL · REPORTS

OF THE

BOARD OF TRUSTEES

OF THE

PUBLIC ₤ LIBRARY

OF THE

CITY OF MILWAUKEE.

OCTOBER 1st, 1892.

MILWAUKEE.
STANDARD PRINTING COMPANY.
1892.

LIBRARY SERVICE.

AUGUST 31, 1892.

MISS THERESA HUBBELL WEST, Deputy Librarian.

REFERENCE DEPARTMENT.

MISS WILLY SCHMIDT, Reference Librarian.
MISS MARY ELVA STILWELL, Assistant and Amanuensis.
WILLIAM JOHN KERSHAW, Evening Assistant.

ISSUING DEPARTMENT.

MISS LUTIE EUGENIA STEARNS, Superintendent.
MISS BELLE BLEND, Assistant.
MISS KARIN SCHUMACHER, Assistant.
MISS JOSEPHINE BUNTESCHU, Assistant.
MISS EMILY LOUISE CORBETT, Assistant.
HARRY BRUCE GRANT, Assistant.
EDWARD ALDEN DONALDSON, Evening Attendant.

READING ROOMS.

MRS. EVA SHEAFE COE, Superintendent.
MISS AGNES SULLIVAN, Assistant.

JANITOR.

HEINRICH SCHWARTZ.

NIGHT WATCHMAN.

DAVID EDWARD DALE.

REPORT OF THE BOARD OF TRUSTEES.

To the Common Council of the City of Milwaukee:

GENTLEMEN:

In accordance with the law establishing in the City of Milwaukee, a Public Library, the Board of Trustees thereof presents herewith its fifteenth annual report, referring you to the accompanying statements of the Acting Librarian for a detailed account of its work and administration during the past year.

From an examination of this report it will be seen that the growth of the library for the period named has been both steady and vigorous, and that public appreciation of the facilities afforded by this institution for study and self-culture has more than kept pace with this growth, the use of the various departments having largely increased during the time covered by the report.

The service performed by the library is especially noticeable in the reference room, the number of daily visitors to this department having increased largely during the past twelve months. Until recently, this branch of the library was not justly appreciated, the general public being unaware that there are to be found here ample means for acquiring information in any branch of science or art of interest to humanity. The acquisition of all the leading works of reference, general and special, that have been published in recent years has greatly increased the utility of this department.

In the Reading Room also the attendance has been arge and constant, the extensive assortment of periodi-

cals of all classes, drawing thither large numbers of our
citizens from all the walks of life,—some seeking recrea-
tion, and others informatiou bearing upon their trades or
professions.

The library is very properly regarded as a branch of
our educational system, and the service it is performing
through the agency of the various public schools, by distributing wholesome literature among the students in attendance, can best be understood by an examination of
the librarian's report.

The system of auxillary delivery stations, established
as an experiment several years ago, has grown in usefull-
ness, until now it has become a very necessary feature.
The cost of the maintenance of these stations in propor-
tion to the number of books issued through them, is high,
but their convenience is daily becoming more generally
recognized by the public at large.

There are now about 65,000 volumes in the library,
and the extensive use made of them warrants the assumption that the generosity ot the city in making this provision for the people, is fully justified.

The acquisition of additional ground for the new
building was exceedingly timely, and the wisdom of the
city in selecting and purchasing this site, has met with
universal commendation. The site is admitted to be the
most beautiful and convenient that could be found in our
beautiful city, and we feel confident that in time our
municipal government will erect a building in every way
worthy of the location.

The need of the new building is daily becoming more
urgent, not only on account of the lack of room which
we now experience, but also on account of the
danger of fire. The library has become exceedingly

valuable, and though it is the endeavor of the Board of Trustees to keep the treasures committed to their charge amply insured, a fire would entail a loss that could not be estimated in dollars and cents. Years of labor are necessary to build up a public library, especially in a city like Milwaukee, where the population is composed of many nationalities engaged in exceedingly diversified pursuits, and where, in consequence, the demands made upon an institution of this sort are also most varied. The danger of fire in a neighborhood of shops, stores and factories, is necessarily great; and though books may escape the flames the damage to them by water is often equally great. It is the sincere wish of the Board of Trustees of the Library that the valuable collection in its keeping may shortly have its own building, where its safety may be assured and its usefulness increased.

For the Board of Trustees of the Public Library,

MATTHEW KEENAN,
President.

REPORT OF THE LIBRARIAN.

MILWAUKEE, October 1st, 1892.

To the Board of Trustees of the Milwaukee Public Library.

GENTLEMEN—In accordance with your rules for the government of this library, I have the honor to submit herewith the reports of the librarian and secretary on the condition and working of the library for the official year ending August 31, 1891, being the fourteenth annual report since the organization of the library.

The most noteworthy facts in the history of the library during the year, outside of the regular routine work of the library, were the tour of inspection of modern library and museum buildings by the joint committee appointed by this board and that of the museum; and the establishment of a bindery in connection with the library. The special report submitted by the committee, Mr. Adolph Meinecke of the museum board and the librarian, gives a detailed statement of their observations and the result in their recommendations for the joint building.

The bindery was established in June, 1891 and the experience of the three months included in this report can hardly be regarded as conclusive, though it seems favorable to the wisdom of the movement.

The statistics of library work for the year, following the same arrangement as that employed in previous reports, are as follows:

BOOKS.

The number of bound volumes in the library at the close of the last report was 52,786. During the year 6,547 volumes were added, of which number 5,397 were acquired by purchase, 474 consisted of pamphlets and magazines bound and placed permanently on the shelves, and the remaining 676 volumes were given to the library by various persons and institutions, a detailed statement of which will be found in Appendix E.

During the same time 354 volumes were worn out and discarded as unserviceable, and 20 volumes were lost and paid for by borrowers. The book account, therefore, at the end of the year, stands as follows:

```
On hand Sept. 1, 1890.................................... .....52,786 vols.
Added up to Aug. 31, 1891.
By gift............ ....................................... 676 vols.
By purchase and exchange................ .....5,397  "
By transfer by binding........................... 474   "
                                      ——————  6,547 vols.

            Total........................................................59,333 vols.
Deduct books discarded............... ........... 354 vols.
Deduct books lost and paid for.............. 20   "
                                      ——————  374 vols.

In the library August 31, 1891.......................... ...........58,959 vols.
```

The number of pamphlets received during the year that have not at once been bound and entered as books is 538, of which 35 were acquired by purchase, while 503 were given to the library according to the detailed statement in Appendix E.

CLASSIFICATION OF ACCESSIONS.

The new books added to the library during the year belong to the following classes:

General and bibliographical works	1,158	17.7
Philosophy and ethics	97	1.5
Religion and theology	268	4.1
Social and political science	720	11.
Philology	70	1.1
Natural science	455	6.9
Useful arts.	339	5.2
Fine arts	220	3.4
Literature in general	321	4.9
Poetry and drama	241	3.7
Prose fiction and children's books	1,490	22.7
History	441	6.7
Geography and travels	360	5.5
Biography	367	5.6
	6,547	100.

Of the of books added to the library the following table shows the number in the various languages:

Volumes in English	5,998	91.6 per cent.
" " German	258	3.9 "
" " French	272	4.2 "
" " Other languages	19	.3 "
Total	6,547	100.

COST OF BOOKS.

The amount expended for books and pamphlets during the year is $8,745.15 which includes $434.08 which was audited and paid on account of books received during the year embraced in the last report. Deducting this amount shows the actual cost of books added to the library during the year to have been $8,311.07.

BINDING.

The number of volumes rebound during the year is 2,339, while 81 were reserved and put back into the old covers. During the same period 768 new books and 517 magazines and newspapers were bound. 1,127 volumes of this number were bound at our own bindery during the three months after its establishment. The amount paid for binding under the contract was $1,319.40, adding to this a bill for $115.50 audited and paid after the close of this report makes the total cost of binding for the year, outside of the newly organized bindery, $1,434.90.

CIRCULATION OF BOOKS.

In Appendix A will be found the usual detailed state-ment of the aggregate circulation of the library by months, and in Appendix B the record of the several delivery stations. This table shows that there were 157,-935 books taken out for home use during the 301.25 working days, a daily average of 524.2.

The date of largest circulation was Jan. 10th when 950 books were issued, the largest number ever given out in one day since the establishment of the library, and the smallest 239, June 16. The month of the highest daily average of issue was June, with an average of 706; and of the lowest, July, with 407.

For comparison a statement of the circulation by months for the last three years is subjoined:

MONTHS.	1888-9.		1889-90.		1890-91.	
	Working days.	Volumes issued.	Working days.	Volumes issued.	Working days.	Volumes issued.
September ...	24	6839	24	7464	25	10215
October	27	8048	27	9731	26	11348
November....	24	8923	25	11832	23	11699
December.....	24	9656	23	11835	24.75	12960
January.......	26	11341	26	13270	25.5	17515
February.....	23	11036	23	13040	23	14512
March.........	26	12589	26	15107	26	15496
April...........	25	13378	26	15189	25.75	14076
May	26	9749	26	13617	25	11149
June............	25	11387	25	13473	26	18360
July	26	8520	26	9752	23.25	10299
August........	24	7579	22	9941	26	10306
Total..........	300	119045	299	144251	301.25	157935
Daily Average.	376.8		482.4		524.2	

Through the delivery stations were sent out 20,870 volumes, and through the schools 15,120, while the branch library at Bay View circulated 2,149. The num, ber of books given out at the main library is 119,796- irrespective of the books used within the library rooms, an increase of 10,497 volumes over the preceding year.

CLASSIFICATION OF CIRCULATION.

The percentages of circulation in the different classes of literature, for the last four years, are as follows:

	1887-8.	1888-9.	1889-90.	1890-91.
General works	4.1	4.2	4.8	4.4
Philosophy	.7	.7	.6	.5
Theology	1.1	.9	1.1	1.1
Social and political science	1.3	1.5	1.2	1.2
Philology	.2	.1	.1	.1
Natural science	1.7	1.9	3.2	4.6
Useful arts	1.6	1.8	1.7	1.7
Fine arts	1.7	1.5	1.7	1.8
Literature in general	5.7	5.3	5.2	5.
Prose fiction	58.2	56.9	48.2	46.2
Children's literature	14.4	14.7	18.9	19.4
History	3.6	4.2	5.3	6.1
Geography and travels	3.5	3.9	5.4	5.3
Biography	2.2	2.4	2.6	2.6

SCHOOL DISTRIBUTION.

The same system of distributing books through the schools in use for two years past has been continued during the present school year. It makes, practically, each school a branch library with a librarian for each thirty or forty children who is, or should be, acquainted with the tastes and needs of each of the children.

The number of books drawn by 93 teachers in 25 schools was 4,096, which were given out 15,120 times, each volume being thus read on an average of 3.7 times while at the schools.

BOOK BORROWERS AND REGISTRATION.

The number of new registrations during the year was 5,171, making the total registration up to the time of the end of this report 46,449. Of this number 35,840 cards have been called in from time to time, after running the designated period of two years, leaving 10,609 now nominally in force. For various causes, such as removal from the city, failure to pay fines, withdrawal of guaranty, etc. 526 cards were cancelled during the year. Of the new cards seventeen were issued in consideration of the stipulated money deposit, and fifteen such deposits were withdrawn. Eight such deposits (this number is from the expert's report to the city) were unreturned at the beginning of the year, thus making ten security deposits on hand at the close of this report.

READING ROOMS.

The total number of visitors to the reading rooms during the 301.25 week days it was open was 51,049, being a daily average of 169. On application at the counter 4,031 magazines were delivered to readers, an average of 13 each day. All other papers and periodicals being kept on tables and racks open to all comers. On 52 Sunday afternoons the number of visitors was 5,859, an average attendance of 113, and 716 magazines or 14 each day were drawn for reading. There have been kept on file during the year 270 serial publications of which 56 may properly be called newspapers and 214 are magazines of general or special interest. The number of magazines is made up of 134 American, 49 English, 25 German, 4 French and 2 Swedish publications. The newspapers comprise 25 dailies and 31 weeklies, semi-monthlies and monthlies, representing the United States, Canada, England, Ireland and Scotland, and Germany. 38 newspapers and 23 magazines are furnished to the library as gifts.

The amount expended for subscriptions is $1,026.63, adding to this amount $61.28 which was audited and paid for German subscriptions belonging to this period after the close of this report, makes the entire cost of subscriptions for the year $1,087.91.

REFERENCE ROOM.

The use of the reference room grows constantly both as to the numbers using the room and the importance of the work done, but no statistics are gathered concerning it.

CATALOGUING.

The cataloguing of the books received during the year has been done by the same force as last year. Four numbers of the Quarterly Index of Additions have been published, of which No. 20 contained a complete list of all the books in the French language which belong to the library, and No. 23 a special list of references on University Extension.

The cost of printing the Quarterlies was $538.15. The amount received from the sale of catalogues and quarterlies is $41.10. In addition to the list of "One Hundred of the Best English Novels" and "One Hundred Good Books for Children" published last year, "A Selection of Good Books for Boys" and "A Selection of Good Books for Girls" have been issued.

ADMINISTRATION.

The library force has remained the same as during the previous year except that the position of Reference Librarian was created, and Miss Willy Schmidt was appointed to the place from the regular force.

16

The cost of maintaining the delivery stations, including the salaries paid to the keepers and the amount paid for cartage to stations and to the schools is $834.57. In May the People's Institute, in whose rooms station F was located, was closed and the station was abandoned. The periodicals were transferred to the Bay View branch on the understanding that a room was to be devoted to library uses.

INSURANCE.

The total insurance carried by the library on its property is $65,000, distributed among the following companies:

Ætna Insurance Co., Hartford	$2,500
Allemania Fire Insurance Co., Pittsburg	2,500
Amazon Insurance Co., Cincinnati	2,500
Boatman's Fire and Marine Insurance Co., Pittsburg	2,500
British America Assurance Co., Toronto	2,500
Buffalo German Insurance Co	2,500
Citizens' Insurance Co., Pittsburg	2,500
Concordia Fire Insurance Co., Milwaukee	5,000
Fire Insurance Co. of the County of Philadelphia	2,500
German Fire Insurance Co. of Peoria, Ill	2,500
Glens Falls Insurance Co., Glens Falls, N. Y	2,500
Insurance Company of North America, Philadelphia	2,500
Michigan Fire and Marine Insurance Co., Detroit	2,500
Milwaukee Mechanics' Insurance Co	5,000
Norwich Union Fire Insurance Society, U. S. Branch, New York	2,500
Pennsylvania Fire Insurance Co., Philadelphia	2,500
Queen Insurance Co., of Liverpool, Western Dep't, Chicago	2,500
Rhode Island Underwriters' Association, Providence	2,500
Rochester German Insurance Co	2,500
Rockford Insurance Co., Rockford, Ill	2,500
Security Insurance Co., New Haven	2,500
Sun Fire Office of London, U. S. Branch, Watertown, N. Y	2,500
Western Assurance Co., Toronto	2,500
Williamsburg City Fire Insurance Co	2,500

FINANCIAL REPORT.

In conclusion I beg leave to submit the usual statement of the receipts and expenditures of the library during the year, including both the miscellaneous receipts of the librarian and the account with the city treasurer, as follows:

CASH ACCOUNT.—1890–91.
RECEIPTS.

Cash on hand Sept. 1, 1890	$ 96.91	
Fines for undue detention of books	457.80	
Catalogues and quarterlies	41.90	
Security deposits	51.00	
Books lost or damaged	35.29	
Lost cards replaced	14.20	
		$697.10

DISBURSEMENTS.

Security deposits refunded	$ 45.00	
Refunded for lost books restored	2.56	
Cash on hand Sept. 1, 1891	649.54	
		$697.10

LIBRARY FUND ACCOUNT.—1890–91.
DEBIT.

Balance in fund Sept., 1890	$10,072.43	
Appropriation for 1891	28,345.72	
		$38,418.15

CREDIT.

Amount of orders drawn for account of

Rent	$ 1,750.00	
Salaries	9,037.62	
Fuel and gas	932.51	
Books	8,745.15	
Newspapers and periodicals	1,026.63	
Postage, express and freight	197.23	
Furniture and repairs	942.78	
Stationery and printing	577.08	
Printing Quarterly additions	538.15	
Insurance	965.00	
Binding	2,134.80	
Delivery stations	834.57	
Building	293.08	
Miscellaneous	653.00	
		$28,627.50

Balance in fund Sept. 1, 1891	$ 9,790.65

All of which is respectfully submitted.

THERESA H. WEST,
Deputy Librarian.

REPORT OF THE LIBRARIAN.

MILWAUKEE, Oct. 1, 1892.

To the Board of Trustees of the Milwaukee Public Library :

GENTLEMEN:—In accordance with your rules for the government of this library, I have the honor to submit herewith the report of the librarian and secretary on the condition and work of the library for the official year ending August 31, 1892, being the fifteenth annual report since the organization of the library. The most important fact in the history of the library during the year 1891–92, was undoubtedly the purchase of the additional ground for the site of the proposed library-museum building. The original site, purchased in 1890, was soon seen to be inadequate for the purpose. Under instructions from the Common Council of the city, conveyed by a resolution adopted unanimously Dec. 14, 1891, the library and museum boards bought lots 14, 15 and 16 and the east thirty feet of lot 13, in block 174, of the Fourth Ward of the city of Milwaukee. Lot 14 and the east thirty feet of lot 13 were bought from Mr. John L. Mitchell for $40,000, and lots 15 and 16 from Mr. E. P. Hackett, the authorized agent of the Birchard estate, for $50,000. This purchase, added to that of 1890, gives as a site the whole frontage of block 174, three hundred feet on Grand avenue between Eighth and Ninth streets, with a depth on Ninth stret of 255 feet and on Eighth street of 150 feet, making as a whole a situation for the joint building hardly equalled, for like purposes, by any city in the country.

The statistics of the library work for the year are largely compiled, as they have been for several years previous, by Miss Willy Schmidt, the reference librarian. The order of arrangement is that adopted in previous reports.

BOOKS.

The number of bound volumes in the library at the close of the last report was 58,959. During the year 5,803 volumes were added, of which number 4,809 volumes were acquired by purchase, 539 volumes consisted of magazines and pamphlets, bound and placed permanently on the shelves, and the remaining 455 volumes were given to the library by various persons and institutions, a detailed statement of which appears in Appendix E. During the same time 526 volumes were worn out and discarded as not fit for further use and 19 volumes were lost and paid for by borrowers. The book account at the end of the year, therefore, stands as follows :

```
On hand Sept. 1, 1891...............................................58,959 vols.
Added up to Aug. 31, 1892.
    By gift.................................................  455 vols.
    By purchase and exchange....................4,809   "
    By transfer by binding.........................  599   "
                                                   ————  5,803 vols.

        Total.............................................       64,762 vols.
    Deduct books discarded........................  526 vols.
    Deduct books lost and paid for............   19   "
                                                   ————    545 vols.

    In the library Aug. 31, 1892................       64,217 vols.
```

The number of pamphlets received during the year that have not been bound at once and entered as books is 541. of which 6 were bought, while 535 were given to the library, as appears in the detailed statement in Appendix E.

CLASSIFICATION OF ACCESSIONS.

The new books added to the library during the year belong to the following classes:

	Volumes.	Percentage.
General and bibliographical works	922	15.9
Philosophy and ethics	70	1.2
Religion and theology	212	3.7
Social and political science	549	9.5
Philology	64	1.1
Natural science	406	7.
Useful arts	373	6.4
Fine arts	153	2.6
Literature in general	447	7.7
Poetry and drama	155	2.7
Prose fiction and children's books	1,670	28.8
History	302	5.2
Geography and travels	210	3.6
Biography	270	4.6
	5,803	100.

The somewhat large percentage of fiction is due to the purchase of some hundreds of volumes of new German literature which were largely novels. Of the whole number of books added to the library the following table shows the number in the various languages:

Volumes in English	4,423	76.2	per cent.
" " German	1,203	20.7	"
" " French	129	2.2	"
" " other languages	48	.9	"
	5,803	100.	

COST OF BOOKS.

The amount expended for books and pamphlets during the year is $8,035.69.

BINDERY.

The report of the bindery is for the fifteen months since its establishment in June, 1891.

DEBIT ACCOUNT.

Cost of machinery and tools	$741.71
" materials	1,043.19
" wages	2,175.73
" rent	300.00
" fuel	23 00
Total	$4,283.63

CREDIT ACCOUNT.

Value of work produced	$3,008.98
" stock on hand	403.55
" machinery and tools	741.71
Total	$4,154.24

The item of rent, which for the fifteen months amounts to $300, will not be a permanent expense in the new building. Deducting this amount from the total expense, $4,283.63, leaves $3,983.63, and deducting this remainder from the credit account, $4,154.24, leaves a balance of $170.61 to the credit of the new bindery.

During the fifteen months covered by this report, 3,667 books have been rebound, while 127 were resewed and put back in the old covers. During the same period 1,039 new books and 520 magazines and newspapers were bound, making a total of 5,353 volumes handled.

The work is promptly and carefully done, and is thus far, extremely satisfactory in all ways. The only question that seems open is whether we shall be able to supply work for as large a force during each year.

CIRCULATION OF BOOKS.

In Appendix A will be found the usual detailed statement of the aggregate circulation of the library by

months, and in Appendix B the record of the several
delivery stations. The main facts which the tables show
are as follows: The total number of books taken out for
use during 285 working days was 151,597, being a daily
average of 531.9 volumes. The date of largest circulation was January 5, when 1,690 volumes were issued, but
this was under unusual circumstances, this being the first
day of opening the library after it was closed during the
alterations made last winter. The next highest circulation was on February 4, with 983 volumes, which is a
legitimate day's work. The day of smallest circulation
was Oct. 6, with 274. The month of highest daily average of issue, 659, was February; and of the lowest, 415,
September.

For comparison, a statement of the circulation by
months, for the last three years is subjoined:

MONTHS.	1889-90.		1890-91.		1891-92.	
	Working days.	Volumes issued.	Working days.	Volumes issued.	Working days.	Volumes issued.
September...	24	7464	25	10215	25	10380
October.......	27	9731	26	11348	27	11252
November....	25	11832	23	11699	24	11535
December.....	23	11835	24.75	12960	20	10764
January	26	13270	25.5	17515	23	13712
February.....	23	13040	23	14512	24	15806
March	26	15107	26	15496	27	16331
April............	26	15189	25.75	14076	26	15693
May	26	13617	25	11149	25	14338
June.............	25	13473	26	18360	26	16372
July.............	26	9752	23.25	10299	25	10490
August........	22	9941	26	10306	13	4924
Total..........	299	144251	301.25	157925	285	151597
Daily average.	482.4		524.2		531.9	

It will be seen from this statement that the daily average of books issued for home use has a steady growth from year to year. The circulation is still by no means so large as it should be in a city of the size of Milwaukee. There seems to be need to bring the knowledge of the treasures of information and inspiration that the library contains to the more practical knowledge of the people.

CLASSIFICATION OF CIRCULATION.

The percentages of circulation in the different classes of literature, for the last five years, are as follows:

	1887-8.	1888-9.	1889-90.	1890-1.	1891-2.
General works	4.1	4.2	4.8	4.4	5.1
Philosophy	.7	.7	.6	.5	.5
Theology	1.1	.9	1.1	1.1	1.
Social and political science.	1.3	1.5	1.2	1.2	1.3
Philology	.2	.1	.1	.1	.1
Natural science	1.7	1.9	3.2	4.6	4.2
Useful arts	1.6	1.8	1.7	1.7	1.9
Fine arts	1.7	1.5	1.7	1.8	1.7
Literature in general	5.7	5.3	5.2	5.	5.
Prose fiction	58.2	56.9	48.2	46.2	47.
Children's literature	14.4	14.7	18.9	19.4	18.5
History	3.6	4.2	5.3	6.1	5.9
Geography and travels	3.5	3.9	5.4	5.3	5.
Biography	2.2	2.4	2.6	2.6	2.8

SCHOOL DISTRIBUTION.

The system of distributing books through the schools described in the last two reports has been continued throughout the school year. The work has not extended as fast as we hoped. This is probably partly due to the need of a larger supply of the books most desired, but still more to the fact of the heavy burden which the regular work of the teacher entails.

When the regular duties are accomplished there is necessarily little time, strength or enthusiasm left for this or any other purely philantrophic work.

The number of books drawn by eighty-eight teachers in twenty-three schools was 4,231, which were given out 12,469 times each volume, thus being read on an average of three times.

BOOK BORROWERS AND REGISTRATION.

The number of new registrations during the year was 5,108, making the total number of names registered up to the close of this report 51,557. Of this number 46,449 cards have been cancelled from time to time, after running the designated period of two years, leaving 10,488 cards now nominally in force. For various other reasons, such as removal from the city, failure to pay fines, etc., 124 cards have been cancelled during the year. Of the new cards twenty-eight were issued in consideration of the stipulated money deposit, adding to this number the ten remaining unpaid at the close of the last report, and subtracting the twenty-one withdrawn during the year, we have seventeen deposits still on hand.

READING ROOMS.

The total number of visitors to the reading room during the 300 week days during which it was open was 61,-702, being a daily average of 206. On application at the counter 5,052 magazines were delivered to readers, an average of seventeen each day, all other papers and periodicals being kept on files and tables, where all comers may have direct access to them. On fifty Sunday afternoons the number of visitors was 5,380, an average attendance of 108, and 715 magazines, or fourteen each day, were drawn for reading.

There are now kept on file 291 serial publications, of which 232 are magazines or weekly papers of general interest, or for special purposes, and fifty-nine newspapers. The number of magazines is made up of 155 American, forty-seven English, twenty-three German, six French and one Swedish publications. The newspapers comprise twenty-nine dailies and thirty weeklies, etc., representing the United States, Canada, England, Ireland and Scotland, and Germany. Thirty-five newspapers and twenty-one magazines are furnished to the library free of charge, a detailed statement of which will be found in Appendix F. The total amount expended on this department for the year is $1,041.50, which includes $61.28 paid on account of subscriptions for the previous year, leaving the actual expense for this year $980.22. This amount includes also the cost of the extra copies of Harper's Magazine, Century, Scribner's, Atlantic, Lippincott's, St. Nicholas, Wide Awake, and Harper's Young People, which are issued for home use in monthly numbers.

REFERENCE ROOM.

It is difficult to make the work of the reference room appear in its proper importance as compared to the rest of the library, from the fact that the very nature of the work forbids the gathering of statistics with regard to it without crippling the work. The policy of the library has been from the beginning to allow visitors to this room the utmost liberty consistent with the safety of the books. Not only are the books properly belonging to the department absolutely free of access to every visitor, but any student may have, from the circulating department, any number of books which he wishes for consultation.

That the Milwaukee people may be safely trusted to use this freedom is demonstrated by the result of the inventory in this room, which shows but six books missing during the eight or ten years, which the inventory covers.

The patient, intelligent help of the reference librarian is a matter of frequent comment by visitors to the room.

An interesting feature of the room is what are known as the "exposition" shelves. Here are placed for one week after they are catalogued all news books added to the library, except fiction. There are many regular visitors who are much disappointed if any irregularity in the book supply causes these shelves to be empty.

CATALOGUING.

The cataloguing of accessions has been done by the same force as before. Only one number of the Quarterly Index has been published, the last number of the third volume, as it was intended to push the reprinting of all the additions to the library since 1885 in the form of a supplement to the main catalogue. Under the present circumstances it is necessary to somewhat defer this supplement, and the printing of the Quarterlies should be resumed.

DELIVERY STATIONS.

The six delivery stations have been maintained throughout the year without change. The total expense, including salaries to the keepers and cartage, has been $885.84. This amount includes the expense of carrying the books to and from the schools also.

ADMINISTRATION.

Several changes have occurred in the library force during the year. Fred. C. Lau, of the circulating department, resigned October 3, 1891, and Harry B. Grant was appointed as his successor, after due examination. Miss Harriet I. White resigned her position as superintendent of the reading room Nov. 1, 1891, and Mrs. Eva S. Coe was transferred from the circulating department to fill the position. After due examination, according to the rules of the Board, Miss Emily Corbett was appointed to the vacancy in the circulating department.

On August 11, 1892, Mr. K. A. Linderfelt was dismissed from the office of librarian, having been suspended April 29, and following that date an examination of the financial transactions of the library, instituted by the city government, disclosed shortages during the prior ten years amounting to $9,095.06. Up to the end of the period included in this report, no successor has been elected, the library remaining in charge of the deputy librarian.

INSURANCE.

The total insurance carried by the library on its property is $78,500, distributed among the following companies:

Ætna Insurance Co., Hartford, Conn	$2,500
Allemania Fire Insurance Co., Pittsburg, Pa	2,500
American Fire Insurance Co., Philadelphia, Pa	2,500
British America Assurance Co., Toronto	2,500
Buffalo German Insurance Co., Buffalo, N. Y	2,500
Citizens' Insuranc: Co., Pittsburg, Pa	2,500
Concordia Fire Insurance Co., Milwaukee	5,000
Detroit Fire and Marine Insurance Co., Detroit	2,500
Fire Insurance Co. of the County of Philadelphia	2,500
German Fire Insurance Co. of Peoria, Ill	2,500
Glens Falls Insurance Co., Glens Falls, N. Y	2,500
Hamburg-Bremen Fire Insurance Co., U. S. Branch, New York	2,500
Insurance Company of North America, Philadelphia	2,500
Jersey City Insurance Co., Jersey City, N. J	2,500
Michigan Fire and Marine Insurance Co., Detroit	2,500
Milwaukee Mechanics' Insurance Co	5,000
Norwich Union Fire Insurance Society, U. S. Branch, New York	2,500
Pennsylvania Fire Insurance Co., Philadelphia	2,500
Queen Insurance Co., of America, Western Dep't, Chicago	2,500

Rhode Island Underwriters' Association, Providence..................... 2,500
Rochester German Insurance Co.. 2,500
Rockford Insurance Co., Rockford, Ill... 2,500
St. Paul Fire and Marine Insurance Co., St. Paul........................ 2,500
Security Insurance Co., New Haven...... 2,500
Sun Fire Office of London, U. S. Branch, Watertown, N. Y........... 2,500
Syndicate Insurance Co., of Minneapolis...... 2,500
Western Assurance Co., Toronto............................... 2,500
Williamsburg City Fire Insurance Co................... 2,500

$77,500

Fireman's Fund, of San Francisco, Cal., on bindery................... $1,000

FINANCIAL REPORT.

In conclusion, I beg leave to submit the usual statement of the receipts and expenditures of the library during the year, including both the miscellaneous receipts of the librarian and the *account with the city treasurer, as follows:

CASH ACCOUNT.—1891-92.

RECEIPTS.

Cash on hand Sept. 1, 1891.....................................$ 649.54
Fines for undue detention of books........................   453.72
Catalogues and Quarterlies....................................   52.50
Security deposits...   81.00
Books lost or damaged..   32.48
Lost cards replaced..   12.30
———— $1,281.54

DISBURSEMENTS.

Security deposits refunded.....................................$ 63.00
Refunded for lost books restored...... ....   5.68
Paid city treasurer.. 1,142.09
Balance cash Sept. 1, 1892....................................   70.77
———— $1,281.54

LIBRARY FUND ACCOUNT.—1891–92.

DEBIT.

Balance in fund Sept. 1, 1891....		$9,790.65
Appropriation for 1892................. ....$28,418.78		
Deposited by Librarian—		

Jan. 5, 1892, Treas. receipt No. 1,660	$700.00	
Feb. 2, " " " " 1,667	87.61	
June 1, " " " " 1,692	54.87	
" 15, " " " " 1,695	50 24	
July 9, " " " " 1,703	61.13	
Aug. 4, " " " " 1,713	45.85	
Sept. 9, " " " " 1,722	142.39	
	——— $1,142.09	
	—————	$29,560.87
		—————
		$39,351.52

CREDIT.

Amount of orders drawn for account of—

Rent ....,..........................$ 2,650.90		
Salaries..	9,489.97	
Fuel and gas.............................	1,530.04	
Books..	8,035.69	
Newspapers and periodicals.........................	1,041.50	
Postage, express and freight.........................	174.62	
Furniture and repairs...................................	1,275.05	
Stationery and printing.................	390.91	
Printing Quarterly additions...........	475.12	
Insurance..	967.50	
Binding	3,436.52	
Delivery stations.................... ....·....	885.84	
Miscellaneous..	540.32	
	—————	$30,893.98
		—————
Balance in fund Sept. 1, 1892.................		$8,457.54

All of which is respectfully submitted.

THERESA H. WEST,

Deputy Librarian.

APPENDIX A.—1890-91.

AGGREGATE CIRCULATION.

	Days open.	General works.	Philosophy.	Theology.	Social and Political Science.	Philology.	Natural Science.	Useful Arts.	Fine Arts.	Literature.	Prose fiction.	Children's fiction.	History.	Geography.	Biography.	Total circulation.	Date and highest circulation.	Date and lowest circulation.	Daily average.	Number of cards issued.	Notices sent.
September, 1890	25	481	61	111	159	24	479	176	171	487	5,047	1,749	802	476	242	10,215	6-563	25-307	409	466	184
October, "	26	476	62	155	196	14	418	190	271	599	5,519	1,829	767	631	232	11,348	7-656	1-379	43	583	186
November, "	23	508	62	156	158	8	225	198	253	643	6,860	1,912	760	654	302	11,699	22-744	21-343	509	532	116
December, "	24.75	579	91	181	174	21	59	213	252	596	6,890	1,970	832	674	317	12,660	27-882	76-362	5.3	441	159
January, 1891	25.5	848	79	193	208	24	944	273	266	897	7,443	3,477	1,116	1,084	469	17,515	10-960	8-361	687	591	178
February, "	23	578	82	177	177	16	742	275	272	785	6,728	2,446	964	818	473	14,512	21-938	3-414	631	614	140
March, "	26	636	64	164	190	16	596	271	287	816	7,138	2,961	906	827	559	15,496	7-946	6-388	596	540	201
April, "	25.75	646	60	151	179	23	660	243	237	717	6,569	2,638	851	746	364	14,678	11-873	22-372	567	447	227
May, "	25	451	18	181	176	12	434	219	188	645	5,316	2,170	587	498	279	11,149	16-852	21-289	446	218	228
June, "	26	883	54	119	127	12	1,580	384	269	711	5,660	3,356	1,412	1,518	330	18,380	6-464	16-239	706	250	235
July, "	23.25	455	84	117	119	11	292	187	172	424	5,474	1,999	435	358	205	10,299	15-583	33-288	467	247	226
August, "	26	479	62	111	106	14	276	172	182	460	5,658	1,982	425	833	177	10,306	22-572	20-288	396	232	180
Total	301.75	6,966	791	1,765	1,919	195	7,225	2,761	2,838	7,810	72,064	30,680	9,638	8,812	4,043	167,935	-960	289	524.2	5,171	2,272
Per cent.		4.4	.5	1.1	1.1	.1	4.6	1.7	1.8	5.	46.2	19.4	6.1	5.3	2.6	100					

CIRCULATION OF DELIVERY STATIONS.

A.—SOUTH SIDE, 1ST AVENUE.

	Days open.	General works.	Philosophy.	Theology.	Social and political science.	Philology.	Natural science.	Useful arts.	Fine arts.	Literature.	Prose fiction.	Children's fiction.	History.	Geography.	Biography.	Total circulation.	Date and highest circulation.	Date and lowest circulation.	Daily average.
September, 1890	25	3	2	2	2		4	9	2	8	156	85	24	10	7	312	10—23	30—3	12
October, "	26	1		2	2		6	6	6	7	198	71	32	17	7	353	8—34	10—4	14
November, "	23	3					5	5	10	7	169	69	26	10		305	1—24	7—5	13
December, "	25	5	4	2			6	6	9	13	217	67	35	25	1	390	30—36	22—6	16
January, 1891	26	7	1	1	6		11	6	11	10	225	90	31	14		404	14—30	12—6	16
February, "	23	5					15	4	6	7	211	96	23	16		389	26—30	2—7	17
March, "	26	10	1	2	1		11	3	3	15	217	136	26	18	2	446	5—28	9—6	17
April, "	26	15	2		2		20	2	2	13	239	137	23	20	1	477	15—32	5—5	18
May, "	25	14	1	5			17	2	7	21	220	111	31	20		445	9—30	12—6	18
June, "	26	16		1	2		24	3	6	20	214	160	52	17	1	518	3—34	2—11	20
July, "	26	25	1		2	1	12	8	7	16	166	149	38	11		435	3—26	20—8	17
August, "	26	14		3	1	2	12	13	7	16	145	127	37	13	9	399	14—25	17—4	15
Total	303	118	14	18	14	3	143	65	72	153	2,377	1,298	378	190	28	4,873		36	16.1
Per cent		2.4	.3	.4	.3	.1	2.9	1.3	1.5	3.1	48.8	26.6	7.8	3.9	.6				

APPENDIX B.—1890-91.

CIRCULATION OF DELIVERY STATIONS—(CONTINUED.)

B.—EAST SIDE.

	Days open	General works	Philosophy	Theology	Social and political science	Philology	Natural Science	Useful arts	Fine arts	Literature	Prose fiction	Children's fiction	History	Geography	Biography	Total circulation	Date and highest circulation	Date and lowest circulation	Daily average
September, 1890	25	12	2	4	5		5	2	4	13	146	27	13	9	2	239	30—19	9—2	10
October, "	26	13	2	5	6		3	1	1	8	147	33	5	8	1	233	8—16	11—4	9
November, "	23	13		4	4	1	2	1	2	9	146	23	17	7	1	229	29—24	24—3	10
December, "	25	4	4	4	4	1	2	6	2	11	122	33	13	7		213	30—24	15—3	9
January, 1891	26	12	1	3	5	5	7	2	4	12	143	36	24	6		254	15—21	27—4	10
February, "	23	5			1	1	8	3	2	18	151	42	18	17	1	263	13—21	16—3	11
March, "	26	14		4	2	4	6	4	3	9	140	32	26	14	1	262	19—21	1—3	10
April, "	26	16	1	2	2	4	6		4	18	137	38	28	5	3	249	9—21	31—3	10
May, "	25	13		3	2	2	1		1	9	132	30	16	4	1	223	3—22	16—1	9
June, "	26		2	4	1		6	1		12	129	33	10	3	3	208	3—22	16—1	8
July, "	26	15	3	5	2		1	2		11	144	34	13	7	1	242	29—18	24—3	9
August, "	26	5	2	3	6		1	1		15	137	47	6	9	2	233	20—13	17—3	9
Total	303	131	17	41	37	1	53	23	27	138	1,674	408	189	96	13	2,848	24		1 9 4
Per cent	4.6	.6	1.4	1.3	.1	1.9	.8	.9	4.8	58.8	14.3	6.6	3.4	.5				

APPENDIX B.—1890-91.

CIRCULATION OF DELIVERY STATIONS—(CONTINUED.)

C.—THIRD STREET.

	Days open.	General works.	Philosophy.	Theology.	Social and political science.	Philology.	Natural science.	Useful arts.	Fine arts.	Literature.	Prose fiction.	Children's fiction.	History.	Geography.	Biography.	Total circulation.	Date and highest circulation.	Date and lowest circulation.	Daily average.
September, 1890	25	15	1	2	2		18	5	7	10	98	110	29	25	8	330	19—29	3—2	13
October, "	26	19	1	2			35	5	10	20	123	152	34	15	5	421	25—37	24—7	16
November, "	23	19		5			35	10	12	10	127	150	61	24	1	454	1—37	14—7	20
December, "	25	20	2				18	7	6	14	122	127	77	22	2	417	30—51	8—6	17
January, 1891	26	17		2	4		24	9	9	16	147	157	61	27	3	476	27—43	3—5	18
February, "	23	25		4			35	11	13	16	154	156	69	34		517	18—40	9—9	22
March, "	26	41	1	5	2		17	10	15	14	145	144	58	43	3	494	10—43	23—4	19
April, "	26	27		2			23	10	4	13	161	195	68	32		541	16—41	6—2	21
May, "	25	15	1	3	1		18	6	6	6	124	129	45	16		378	29—39	18—2	15
June, "	26	28		2			19	4	5	6	125	137	35	12		375	6—40	2—5	14
July, "	26	20			3		30	8	3	3	87	95	48	6	8	306	29—30	27—2	12
August, "	26	12			7	1	27	7	3	8	71	84	25		16	268	12—25	17—2	10
Total	303	258	6	27	31		299	92	96	133	1,484	1,636	610	264	40	4,977	51	2	
Per cent		5.2	.1	.5	.6		6.0	1.8	1.9	2.7	29.8	32.9	12.3	5.3	.8				

CIRCULATION OF DELIVERY STATIONS—(CONTINUED.)

D.—WALNUT STREET.

	Days open	General works	Philosophy	Theology	Social and political science	Philology	Natural science	Useful arts	Fine arts	Literature	Prose fiction	Children's fiction	History	Geography	Biography	Total circulation	Date and highest circulation	Date and lowest circulation	Daily average
September, 1890	25	2	..	2	3	..	13	5	5	8	166	45	17	13	6	285	30–27	25–3	11
October, "	26	1	2	3	..	..	11	5	3	7	170	27	31	9	1	272	23–20	18–3	10
November, "	23	1	..	4	3	..	11	8	8	8	127	34	42	10	..	255	25–29	11–3	11
December, "	25	3	..	2	2	..	15	5	7	9	147	66	40	2	..	297	31–25	15–2	12
January, 1891	26	8	..	2	3	..	15	6	6	13	156	70	33	10	..	319	10–28	5–4	12
February, "	23	9	1	..	1	..	18	6	3	9	144	66	28	8	..	291	25–32	21–5	13
March, "	26	5	..	7	6	..	15	8	1	10	156	75	21	12	4	320	27–23	16–2	12
April, "	26	8	2	3	2	..	8	10	5	11	149	74	38	10	..	316	7–27	27–5	12
May, "	25	8	1	3	..	..	8	8	1	7	123	72	25	6	..	269	5–25	4–5	11
June, "	26	7	..	4	3	..	13	6	2	2	118	86	25	10	..	275	3–22	26–4	11
July, "	26	13	..	..	..	..	17	7	3	3	108	56	26	6	4	244	15–19	20–3	11
August, "	26	11	..	1	4	..	17	6	5	8	97	66	8	9	1	233	14–22	24–4	9
Total	303	76	6	31	32	..	162	81	40	95	1,661	737	334	105	16	3,876	32		211.1
Per cent		2.3	.2	.9	.9	..	4.8	2.4	1.2	2.8	49.2	21.8	9.9	3.1	.5				

APPENDIX B.—1890-91.

CIRCULATION OF DELIVERY STATIONS—(CONTINUED).

E.—BAY VIEW.

	Days open.	General works.	Philosophy.	Theology.	Social and political science.	Philology.	Natural science.	Useful arts.	Fine arts.	Literature.	Prose fiction.	Children's fiction.	History.	Geography.	Biography.	Total circulation.	Date and highest circulation.	Date and lowest circulation.	Daily average.
September, 1890	25				2		4	1	1	1	36	15	5	1		65	23—7	22—1	3
October, "	26						1	1	1	3	46	16	9	1		77	1—5	2—1	3
November, "	23	2		1			2	1	1	3	52	6	10	2	1	76	26—8	28—1	3
December, "	25	10		2				3	3	3	56	12	9	4		85	13—8	2—1	3
January, 1891	26	7		2	1		2	2	1	1	46	17	11	1		101	28—14	9—1	4
February, "	23	4						1	3	3	57	13	12	2	2	98	25—11	2—1	4
March, "	26	1		2	1			1	1	1	53	7	3	1		78	12—7	7—1	3
April, "	25	7		2	1				1	3	49	7	19	2		86	5—9	4—1	3
May, "	26	1		1	1		6	4	4	4	58	7	13	1		78	13—16	16—1	3
June, "	26						11	4	2	5	58	36	36	3	3	165	9—12	31—1	6
July, "	26	7		1	2		10	2	1	2	50	51	24	3	3	155	17—9	3—2	6
August, "	26	4		2	2			2	1	6	37	25	16	3	2	107			4
Total	303	40		12	7		36	24	12	31	593	217	167	24	8	1,171	16	1	3.9
Per cent		3.4		1.	.6		3.1	2.1	1.	2.6	50.6	18.5	14.3	2.1	.7				

CIRCULATION OF DELIVERY STATIONS—(CONTINUED.)

F.—GRAND OPERA HOUSE.

	Days open.	General works.	Philosophy.	Theology.	Social and political science.	Philology.	Natural science.	Useful arts.	Fine arts.	Literature.	Prose fiction.	Children's fiction.	History.	Geography.	Biography.	Total circulation.	Date and highest circulation.	Date and lowest circulation.	Daily average.
September, 1890	26			1	2		6		1	3	74	2	13	8	2	112	11— 7	20— 2	4
October, "	26				5		1	2		3	69	13	8	7		108	16— 8	31— 3	4
November, "	23				7		3	2		1	61	5	5	2		86	1— 5	6— 2	4
December, "	25	1			6			1	1	1	59	10	2	1		83	31— 9	1— 2	3
January, 1891	26				5		1			2	53	12	5	1		81	7—14	16— 1	3
February, "	23				4		1			4	38	6	6			53	6— 6	9— 1	2
March, "	26	1						2			29	3	1			36	14— 4	2— 1	1
April, "	10						1				9					11	1— 3	3— 1	1
May, "																			
June, "																			
July, "																			
August, "																			
Total	185	2		1	29		13	7	2	13	392	49	41	19	2	570		14	1
Per cent		.4		.2	5.1		2.2	1.2	.4	2.2	68.8	8.6	7.2	3.3	.4				3.1

APPENDIX B.—1890-91.

CIRCULATION OF DELIVERY STATIONS—(CONTINUED.)

G.—SOUTH SIDE, GROVE STREET.

	Days open	General works	Philosophy	Theology	Social and political science	Philology	Natural science	Useful arts	Fine arts	Literature	Prose fiction	Children's fiction	History	Geography	Biography	Total circulation	Date and highest circulation	Date and lowest circulation	Daily average
September, 1890	25			4	1		7	4	1	6	83	39	12	9	2	168	8—11	22—2	7
October, "	26	2		3	1		9	8	4	4	106	53	17	3	3	213	8—13	20—1	8
November, "	23		1	1	2		6	7	4	8	88	25	15	6	1	166	26—14	8—1	7
December, "	25	1		6	3		6	6	2	8	107	27	30	6		202	30—17	23—2	8
January, 1891	26	2	1	2	3		8	8	6	11	107	43	27	2	3	223	23—19	20—3	9
February, "	23	14		2	3		17	9	4	14	119	71	16	10	4	272	25—30	3—3	12
March, "	26	8	1	9	3		8	19	2	15	141	74	30	8	1	320	1—28	9—4	12
April, "	26	7		3	2		9	6	2	10	168	68	27	8		319	1—22	20—6	12
May, "	25	7	1	5	1		8	2	2	10	131	81	11	4	2	262	6—24	12—3	10
June, "	26	8		5	3		14	5	2	5	130	104	14	6		295	26—21	1—2	11
July, "	26		2	4	4		15	5	8	7	128	117	33	9	1	334	7—31	2—4	13
August, "	26	14		2	2		10	8	8	9	132	77	11	9		281	22—19	13—4	11
Total	303	63	8	41	29		117	86	43	107	1,440	779	245	80	17	3,055	31	1	10
Per cent		2.1	.3	1.4	1.		3.9	2.8	1.4	3.2	47.2	25.58		2.6	.6				

APPENDIX B—(CONTINUED).—1890-91.

CIRCULATION OF BAY VIEW BRANCH LIBRARY.

	Days open.	General works.	Philosophy.	Theology.	Social and political science.	Philology.	Natural science.	Useful arts.	Fine arts.	Literature.	Prose fiction.	Children's fiction.	History.	Geography.	Biography.	Total circulation.	Date and highest circulation.	Date and lowest circulation.	Daily average.
September, 1890	25			1						6	105	19	1	3	4	139	29—10	26—1	6
October, "	26	1	1							9	104	29	9	2	7	161	7—18	2—3	6
November, "	23		1	2						7	112	31	4	6	8	170	22—15	13—1	7
December, "	25	2	1				1			3	146	21	4	2	6	186	27—19	3—2	7
January, 1891	26		1							9	120	23	6	8	4	172	10—13	23—1	7
February, "	23	3	1	2						7	109	22	6	3	3	152	7—13	17—2	7
March, "	26	4	1	2						6	141	29	5	3	10	200	21—21	30—2	8
April, "	26	1					2			8	150	26	9	9	8	218	20—18	24—1	8
May, "	25									11	126	17	4		7	166	2—17	26—1	7
June, "	26			3						12	137	24	2	2	4	186	1—17	30—2	7
July, "	26			1						8	146	27	4	7	3	195	11—12	9—3	8
August, "	26						1			12	148	30	8	4	1	204	29—13	4—4	8
Total	303	11	6	11			4			98	1,544	298	62	50	65	2,149	21	1	7.1
Per cent		.5	.3	.5			.2			4.6	71.8	13.9	2.9	2.3	3.				

APPENDIX B—Continued.—1890-91.

CIRCULATION THROUGH SCHOOLS.

	General works.	Philosophy.	Theology.	Social and political science.	Philology.	Natural science.	Useful arts.	Fine arts.	Literature.	Prose fiction.	Children's fiction.	History.	Geography.	Biography.	Total circulation.
September, 1890															
October, "															
November, "															
December, "	253		2	3	1	166	40	13	7	7	228	63	58		532
January, 1891	59			19	10	507	25	5	100	98	1,572	335	372	90	393
February, "	29			4	2	195	9	7	62	3	263	81	153	50	917
March, "	103		6	22	4	64	22	5	50	14	263	102	90	33	679
April, "	22			12	6	200	2		31	4	296	57	129	17	898
May, "			7	34		88		88	21	22	358	32	99	18	674
June, "	445			7	15	1,280	139		247	293	3,327	878	1,134	140	8,027
July, "															
August, "															
Total	911		19	100	38	2,500	237	118	518	441	6,307	1,548	2,035	348	15,120
Per cent	6.		.1	.7	.3	16.5	1.6	.8	3.4	2.9	41.7	10.2	13.5	2.3	

APPENDIX C.—1890-91.

READING ROOM.

	DAYS OPEN.		READERS.			MAGAZINES.			DAILY AVERAGE.			
---	---	---	---	---	---	---	---	---	READERS.		MAGAZINES.	
	Sec. days.	Sun-days.	Secular days.	Sun-days.	Total.	Secular days.	Sun-days.	Total.	Secular days.	Sun-days.	Secular days.	Sun-days.
September, 1890	25	4	4,058	412	4,470	293	60	353	162	103	12	15
October, "	26	4	4,334	496	4,830	354	71	425	167	124	14	18
November, "	23.75	5	4,171	673	4,844	296	74	370	181	135	13	15
December, "	24.75	4	4,662	615	5,277	365	72	437	188	154	15	18
January, 1891	25.5	4	5,463	479	5,942	388	52	440	214	120	15	13
February, "	23	4	4,485	524	5,009	378	68	446	195	131	16	17
March, "	26	5	4,592	602	5,194	393	72	465	177	120	15	14
April, "	25.75	4	3,994	444	4,438	369	63	432	155	111	15	16
May, "	25	5	3,512	528	4,040	303	63	366	140	105	12	13
June, "	26	4	3,782	341	4,123	335	44	379	145	85	13	11
July, "	25.25	4	3,395	381	3,776	251	28	279	134	95	10	7
August, "	26	5	4,601	364	4,965	306	49	355	177	73	12	10
Total	301.25	52	51,049	5,859	56,908	4,031	716	4,747	169	113	13	14

APPENDIX E.

1890–91.

LIST OF GIFTS TO THE LIBRARY.

	Volumes.	Pamphlets.
Aberdeen, Scotland, public library................		1
Aguilar free library society, New York, N. Y................		1
Albany, N. Y., Cathedral of All Saints', Diocesan lend-		
ing library.....................		1
American bankers' association, New York, N. Y..........		1
American bar association, Philadelphia, Penn............		1
American unitarian association, Boston, Mass............		1
Amherst, Mass., college..		3
Ball, N., Block Island, R. I............		2
Beloit, Wis., college...		1
Birch's Sons, T., Philadelphia, Penn......	1	
Boston, Mass., Ladies commission on Sunday-school		
books..		4
Boston, Mass., public library.......................................		6
Bowdoin college, Brunswick, Me............		1
Bowes, J. L., Liverpool, England......	1	1
Bradley, Mrs. W. H., Milwaukee......................		53
Brigham, W. T., Baltimore................ ,........................	1	
Bronson library, Waterbury, Conn.............................		2
Brookline, Mass., public library...................................		1
Brooklyn, N. Y., library...		3
" " union for christian work...................		1
Brown, J. C., Haddington, Scotland............................		2
Brown university, Providence, R. I......		2
Brymner, D., Ottawa, Canada..................................	1	
Buffalo, N. Y., library..		1
California, state library, Sacramento, Cal.................	3	
" " mining bureau, Sacramento, Cal.......		3
" university, Berkeley, Cal.............................		1
Cambridge, Mass., public library.................................		1
Canada, Royal society of, Montreal, Canada.............	2	

42

47

676   503

APPENDIX A.—1891-92.
AGGREGATE CIRCULATION.

	Days open	General works	Philosophy	Theology	Social and Political science	Philology	Natural science	Useful arts	Fine arts	Literature	Prose fiction	Children's fiction	History	Geography	Biography	Total circulation	Date and highest circulation	Date and lowest circulation	Daily average	Number of cards issued	Notices sent
September, 1891	25	429	66	102	117	22	394	208	185	484	5,276	1,887	515	481	284	10,880	12-588	24-321	415	310	222
October, "	27	512	80	124	155	26	328	213	246	608	5,887	1,846	569	898	280	11,252	31-837	6-274	417	458	201
November, "	24	591	62	104	155	12	357	229	198	624	5,768	1,915	633	507	370	11,535	28-730	11-337	481	506	199
December, "	26	691	47	110	141	13	533	227	139	541	4,866	1,935	598	645	288	10,764	5-828	3-2-3	538	388	187
January, 1892	23	711	69	144	167	19	642	276	256	791	6,548	2,190	793	729	389	13,712	5-1090	14-337	596	547	172
February, "	24	838	82	166	175	22	907	332	311	937	6,909	2,700	1,030	867	510	15,806	27-983	5-1690	605	742	218
March, "	27	866	88	193	220	23	578	341	300	928	7,460	2,840	1,126	847	523	16,831	5-947	30-32	659	725	278
April, "	26	771	77	163	201	9	1,017	243	251	773	7,329	3,188	865	822	426	15,603	2-918	27-367	605	388	503
May, "	25	750	79	133	213	13	166	292	218	696	6,126	2,726	798	950	371	14,838	7-724	5-306	608	341	328
June, "	28	803	51	186	201	12	773	269	232	615	6,445	3,793	1,468	1,023	471	16,372	4-825	16-296	630	260	333
July, "	25	46?	57	73	11	13	289	201	171	408	5,811	2,054	424	282	185	10,490	9-568	28-306	420	292	294
August, "	13	217	32	81	51	9	99	71	82	150	2,963	898	167	180	124	4,924	13-596	9-281	379	136	415
Total	285	7,640	790	1,629	1,807	198	6,423	2,88?	2,578	7,578	71,268	27,972	8,996	7,831	4,231	151,597	1,690	274	531.9	5,106	3,140
Per cent		5.1	.5	1.	1.3	.1	4.2	1.9	1.7	5.	47.	18.5	5.9	5.	2.8	100.					

APPENDIX B.

CIRCULATION OF DELIVERY STATIONS.

A.—SOUTH SIDE, 1st AVENUE.

	Days open	General works	Philosophy	Theology	Social and political science	Philology	Natural science	Useful arts	Fine arts	Literature	Prose fiction	Children's fiction	History	Geography	Biography	Total circulation	Date and highest circulation	Date and lowest circulation	Daily average
September, 1891	25	20			2		9	10	4	13	173	134	22	10	8	405	9—22	11—10	16
October, "	27	20		1			8	11	10	15	196	122	19	7	5	414	28—24	15— 9	15
November, "	24	15			4		2	14	2	8	190	104	26	13	3	377	27—31	23— 6	16
December, "	20	21					4	9	7	9	167	65	33	14	5	333	19—31	21— 2	17
January, 1892	23	28			2		9	14	1	11	197	107	30	7	1	413	5—101	11— 6	18
February, "	24	20		3	5		14	10	5	13	153	114	19	11	4	369	27—25	29— 5	15
March, "	27	26			3		18	5	1	14	204	129	36	15	1	462	5—31	21— 7	17
April, "	26	37		1	3		14	6	8	15	238	148	28	11	6	512	30—40	1—20	20
May, "	25	30			2		15	13	3	8	192	113	25	8	4	408	18—27	16— 4	16
June, "	26	21		2	5		25	6	6	4	198	141	24	6	7	445	1—44	2— 6	17
July, "	25	6		2			27	13	4	15	151	107	37	9	3	375	7—28	18— 6	15
August, "	13	10		1	1		3	1	4	8	59	41	10	1	4	143	8—15	1— 3	11
Total	285	254		9	31		148	110	56	133	2,118	1,325	309	112	51	4,656	101		216.3
Per cent		5.4		.2	.7		3.2	2.4	1.2	2.8	45.5	28.5	6.6	2.4	1.1	100			

CIRCULATION OF DELIVERY STATIONS—(CONTINUED.)

B.—EAST SIDE.

	Days open.	General works.	Philosophy.	Theology.	Social and political science.	Philology.	Natural science.	Useful arts.	Fine arts.	Literature.	Prose fiction.	Children's fiction.	History.	Geography.	Biography.	Total circulation.	Date and highest circulation.	Date and lowest circulation.	Daily average.
September, 1891	25	10	2	2	2		1	2	3	11	151	25	11	8	7	235	19—16	8—4	9
October, "	27	8	1	2	2		2	3	2	13	149	38	18	10		248	28—18	30—3	9
November, "	24	9	5					5		16	114	29	8	6	4	196	17—17	2—2	8
December, "	20	5	4	3	3	2	3	3			87	28	4	4	1	149	2—12	18—1	7
January, 1892	23	5	8		3	2	3	3	3	6	128	30	17	10	4	221	5—46	11—3	10
February, "	24	11	11	3	2		2	4	3	7	110	28	8	4	5	200	25—20	26—2	8
March, "	27	18	1	4			5	4	5	12	138	24	17	18	7	263	31—17	1—?	10
April, "	26	13	4	3	1		4		4	14	145	40	9	10	11	257	28—24	1—4	10
May, "	25	10	3	2			3	3	4	14	123	33	14	9	8	218	26—18	28—2	8
June, "	26	16	2	1	3		5	1	4	8	130	44	12	4	2	231	1—21	16—1	9
July, "	25	6	2	2	2		3	4	2	8	105	33	14	5	1	186	20—19	25—1	7
August, "	13	5		1			1	1	1	6	65	12	2	2	1	99	6—15	15—2	7
Total	285	118	45	20	17	4	32	33	31	119	1,445	364	134	90	51	2,503	46	1	8
Per cent		4.7	1.8	.8	.7	.2	1.3	1.3	1.2	4.8	57.7	14.5	5.4	3.62	5.				8

APPENDIX B.

CIRCULATION OF DELIVERY STATIONS. (Continued).

C.—THIRD STREET.

	Days open	General works	Philosophy	Theology	Social and political science	Philology	Natural science	Useful arts	Fine arts	Literature	Prose fiction	Children's fiction	History	Geography	Biography	Total circulation	Date and highest circulation	Date and lowest circulation	Daily average
September, 1891	25	10			1		4	9	3	3	83	147	26	10	2	298	30—29	7—1	12
October, "	27	21			1		11	5	4	1	93	111	40	10		297	7—33	30—3	11
November, "	24	24		1	1		14	3	7	5	98	87	27	11	2	280	3—28	23—2	12
December, "	20	19					21	1	2	3	86	86	27	9	5	260	16—28	21—4	11
January, 1892	23	29	1	1	5		37	3	6	5	115	66	47	7	3	325	5—69	11—4	14
February, "	24	20		1	2		31	4	7	9	103	66	26	18	4	291	29—22	1—4	12
March, "	27	28	2	3	2		35	2	5	11	118	57	30	14	12	317	15—27	28—3	12
April, "	26	21		3	7		24	1	1	9	110	54	23	13	8	286	7—25	12—4	11
May, "	25	13		3	2		19	4	7	19	62	46	21	22	8	226	11—20	17—1	9
June, "	26	10		2	3		8	1	8	6	70	59	12	16	10	200	11—16	1—2	8
July, "	25	8		1	3		8	6	6	9	56	39	21	4	1	159	6—14	5—1	6
August, "	13	4			2		5	1	3	2	27	20	5			74	3—12	1—2	6
Total	285	207	3	15	28		213	38	69	81	1,021	838	305	138	54	3,013	69		10.6
Per cent		6.9	.1	.5	.9		7.1	1.2	2.3	2.7	33.9	27.8	10.1	4.6	1.8				

APPENDIX B.

CIRCULATION OF DELIVERY STATIONS.—(CONTINUED.)

D.—WALNUT STREET.

	Days open.	General works.	Philosophy.	Theology.	Social and political science.	Philology.	Natural science.	Useful arts.	Fine arts.	Literature.	Prose fiction.	Children's fiction.	History.	Geography.	Biography.	Total circulation.	Date and highest circulation.	Date and lowest circulation.	Daily average.
September, 1891	25	11			1		4	4	2	11	94	75	18	5		225	11—25	30—2	9
October, "	27	9		3	4		5	4	2	2	109	58	20	5		229	2—17	26—4	8
November, "	24	5		1	5		6	3		6	97	47	7	10	2	189	10—14	3—2	8
December, "	20	4			5		4	3	3	10	82	38	13	4		165	17—17	3—2	8
January, 1892	23	16		1	16		13	5		22	117	50	28	11	2	279	5—47	9—1	12
February, "	24	12			6		13	5	1	15	105	34	20	10	2	223	25—18	15—5	9
March, "	27	12		2	6		12	1	4	20	125	41	12	7	4	245	19—19	29—2	9
April, "	26	13			3		15	5		8	94	25	13	11	1	184	6—13	18—2	7
May, "	25	18			5		6		2	15	95	22	18	11	1	188	19—12	6—2	7
June, "	26	11	1	1	5	2	7	1	2	9	116	29	20	3	7	211	1—17	24—2	8
July, "	25	2			3		9		2	9	66	28	24			148	22—14	18—1	6
August, "	13	6					1			4	37	13	4	1	1	67	11—11	1—3	5
Total	285	119	1	9	59	2	95	26	18	139	1137	460	197	68	23	2.353	47	1	8.3
Per cent	...5.		.1	.4	2.5	.14		1.1	.8	5.9	48.3	19.5	8.4	2.91					

APPENDIX B.

CIRCULATION OF DELIVERY STATIONS.—(Continued).

E.—BAY VIEW.

	Days open.	General works.	Philosophy.	Theology.	Social and political science.	Philology.	Natural science.	Useful arts.	Fine arts.	Literature.	Prose fiction.	Children's fiction.	History.	Geography.	Biography.	Total circulation.	Date and highest circulation.	Date and lowest circulation.	Daily average.
September, 1891	25	1			1				1	3	34	22	13	3	3	87	21— 7	7-30—1	3
October, "	27	1	8	5			1		2	1	49	11	11	5		94	24— 6	2—1	4
November, "	24	3	1	1	5		3		1	1	47	10	14	3	3	87	28— 8	8-20—1	4
December, "	20		1	3	4						56	5	1	3	1	75	19— 8	8-18—1	4
January, 1892	23			5			2			2	73	14	13	5		119	5—20	7-20—1	5
February, "	24	1	1	6	1		3	1	4	3	71	23	7	3		112	24—16	9—1	4
March, "	27						1			1	105	20	11	1	1	152	22—11	31—2	6
April, "	26			2				3		3	85	16	7	2		119	22—10	25—1	4
May, "	25		1	2	6		1	1		4	87	14	7	3	2	117	24—10	13—1	5
June, "	26		2	1						2	80	20	4		1	120	3—11	17—1	5
July, "	25	2	1	1	1		1	1	1		73	11	6			102	6— 8	25—2	4
August, "	13						1			4	40	7	4			52	12— 9	11—1	4
Total	285	8	15	26	18		22	7	9	24	800	173	98	28	8	1,236	20	1	
Per cent		.6	1.2	2.1	1.5		1.8	.6	.7	2.	64.7	14.	7.9	2.3	.6				4.3

APPENDIX B.

CIRCULATION OF DELIVERY STATIONS—(CONTINUED.)

G.—SOUTH SIDE, GROVE STREET.

	Days open.	General works.	Philosophy.	Theology.	Social and political science.	Philology.	Natural science.	Useful arts.	Fine arts.	Literature.	Prose fiction.	Children's fiction.	History.	Geography.	Biography.	Total circulation.	Date and highest circulation.	Date and lowest circulation.	Daily average.
September, 1891	25	11	1	....	1	1	2	6	4	1	144	72	13	1	....	257	2–20	14–3	10
October, "	27	14	....	....	1	1	6	7	9	4	140	47	20	7	1	257	21–18	8–3	10
November, "	24	9	....	1	2	....	....	5	5	8	121	62	19	11	1	252	17–17	9–3	10
December, "	20	12	....	....	....	....	9	6	1	....	120	39	13	14	....	225	11–22	5–4	11
January, 1892	23	9	....	1	....	....	14	9	9	17	164	85	26	19	2	354	5–93	11–4	15
February, "	24	16	2	3	1	....	10	3	1	9	168	58	27	9	3	310	24–32	9–5	13
March, "	27	26	1	4	2	....	14	1	7	16	184	59	27	6	5	352	5–27	15–3	13
April, "	26	26	4	1	1	....	4	4	2	10	172	82	28	5	2	341	9–22	22–2	12
May, "	25	33	....	....	4	....	5	3	4	4	193	67	12	5	....	331	21–20	2–5	13
June, "	26	33	1	....	1	....	14	4	4	10	173	100	33	9	4	390	3–31	6–5	15
July, "	25	9	....	....	....	....	13	5	7	11	125	53	26	5	1	259	9–19	12–4	10
August, "	13	8	....	2	....	1	1	3	6	5	53	19	13	1	....	110	2–15	9–3	9
Total	285	206	9	11	13	2	99	64	59	107	1,760	743	257	87	21	3,438	93		2
Per cent		6.	.3	.3	.4	.1	2.9	1.9	1.7	3.1	51.2	21.4	7.5	2.6	.6				12.1

APPENDIX B. (CONTINUED).
CIRCULATION OF BAY VIEW BRANCH LIBRARY.

	Days open	General works	Philosophy	Theology	Social and political science	Philology	Natural science	Useful arts	Fine arts	Literature	Prose fiction	Children's fiction	History	Geography	Biography	Total circulation	Date and highest circulation	Date and lowest circulation	Daily average
September, 1891	25			2						6	134	20	9	1	1	173	22—14	23—1	7
October, "	27	18	1							9	147	14	1	2		192	20—14	7—3	8
November, "	24	5		1						8	104	16	4	9	8	155	27—13	18—1	6
December, "	20			1						9	111	12	3	5	6	147	16—16	18—	7
January, 1892	23	6		1					1	7	152	10	7	1	11	196	5—76	6—2	8
February, "	24	2		2		1				18	116	14	6	4	6	170	5—15	2—2	7
March, "	27			6		2	1			27	133	24	6	9	6	212	28—17	30—3	8
April, "	26			3	2		2			9	157	27	2	2	1	211	9—17	22—	8
May, "	25				1	1	1			10	109	25	6	4	5	156	2—15	24—1	6
June, "	26			1	1					6	108	19		4		144	22—11	29—1	6
July, "	25			1			3		1	1	103	21				134	30—10	14—1	5
August, "	13									3	43	11		1	1	58	12—10	6—1	4
Total	285	31	1	17	4	4	7		2	113	1,417	213	44	44	54	1,948	76		
Per cent	1.6	.1	.9	.2	.2	.3		.1	5.8	72.7	10.9	2.3	2.3	2.8				6.8

APPENDIX B. (Continued.)

CIRCULATION THROUGH SCHOOLS.

1891—1892.

	General works.	Philosophy.	Theology.	Social and political science.	Philology.	Natural science.	Useful arts.	Fine arts.	Literature.	Prose fiction.	Children's fiction.	History.	Geography.	Biography.	Total circulation.
September, 1891											15				15
October, "														70	70
November, "													158	27	1,019
December, "	126			11		209	20	1	13	7	354	94	158	27	1,019
January, 1892	44			1		196	5	1	41	4	156	64	146	47	705
February, "	142			1		250	20	28	83	16	408	184	147	41	1,304
March, "	58					26	12	7	7	16	186	235	97	3	640
April, "	115	2		4		128	14	13	93	65	699	153	170	14	1470
May, "	113			8		651	26		41	4	791	275	502	79	2490
June, "	229		84	14		488	80	36	195	86	1859	990	650	225	4936
July, "															
August, "															
Total	827	2	84	39		1,948	177	78	473	182	4468	1,995	1,870	506	12649
Per cent	6.5	.1	.7	.3		15.4	1.4	.6	3.7	1.4	35.3	15.8	14.8	4.	

APPENDIX C.

READING ROOM.

| | DAYS OPEN. | | READERS. | | | MAGAZINES. | | | DAILY AVERAGE. | | | |
| | | | | | | | | | READERS. | | MAGAZINES. | |
	Sec. days.	Sun-days.	Secular days.	Sun-days.	Total.	Secular days.	Sun-days.	Total.	Secular days.	Sun-days.	Secular days.	Sun-days.
September, 1891	26	4	2,651	433	3,084	243	35	278	102	108	9	9
October, "	27	4	3,921	409	4,330	344	46	390	145	102	13	11
November, "	24	5	6,065	669	6,734	356	63	419	252	134	15	13
December, "	20	3	5,303	440	5,743	322	57	379	265	150	16	19
January, 1892	23	4	5,442	584	6,026	415	53	468	237	146	18	13
February, "	24	4	6,598	511	7,109	517	80	597	275	128	22	20
March, "	27	4	7,682	526	8,208	598	87	685	284	131	22	22
April, "	26	4	6,182	514	6,696	530	90	620	238	128	20	23
May, "	25	5	4,886	523	5,409	489	73	562	195	104	20	15
June, "	26	4	4,829	269	5,088	450	53	503	186	65	18	13
July, "	25	5	3,676	304	3,980	369	49	418	147	60	15	10
August, "	27	4	4,467	208	4,675	419	29	448	165	52	16	8
Total	300	50	61,702	5,380	67,082	5,052	715	5,767	206	108	17	14

APPENDIX D.

COMPARATIVE SUMMARY OF STATISTICS.

	1890-91.	1891-92.
Books in Library, beginning of year	52,786	58,959
Total accessions	6,547	5,803
Given	676	455
Transferred by binding	474	539
Purchased	5,397	4,809
Cost of books actually received	$8,745.15	$8,035.69
Worn out and discarded	354	526
Lost, sold and exchanged	20	19
Pamphlets, accessions	486	541
Registered book borrowers, beginning of year	41,278	46,449
New names registered	5,171	5,108
Circulation of books	157,935	151,597
Working days	301.25	285
Daily average	524.2	531.9
Largest issue in one day	950	1,690
Smallest issue in one day	239	274
Number of books fined	2,272	3,140
Received for fines	$457.80	$453.72
Reading room—Magazines on file	214	232
Newspapers on file	56	59
Visitors	51,049	61,702
Days open	301.25	300
Average daily attendance	169	206
Magazines delivered	4,031	5,052
Sunday readers	5,859	5,380
Sundays open	52	50
Average attendance on Sundays	113	108
Magazines delivered	716	715
Cost of serials	$1,026.63	$1,217.27
Binding and repairing—number volumes	2,682	
Cost of binding and repairing	$1,319.40	$4,283.63
Appropriation, 1891, 1892	$28,345.72	$28,418.78
Amount paid for salaries	$9,037.62	$9,489.97

The reports for binding for 1890–91 and 1891–92 are divided between the two binderies, that for 1891–92 including the three months' work by our own bindery before the beginning of this report.

APPENDIX E.

1891–92.

LIST OF GIFTS TO THE LIBRARY.

	Volumes.	Pamphlets
Aberdeen, Scotland, public library		1
Adsit, Mrs. C. D., Milwaukee.		1
American historical association, Washington, D. C....	1	
American library association, Boston, Mass.		1
Amherst, Mass., college		1
Baer & Co., Jos., Frankf. a. M., Germany	1	
Benzenberg, J., Milwaukee	15	
Berry, J. M., Worcester, Mass.		1
Birch's Sons, T., Philadelphia, Penn	1	1
Birmingham, England, free libraries		1
Boston, Mass., public library	1	3
Bradley, Mrs. W. H., Milwaukee		10
Bridgman, H. B., New York, N. Y.	1	
Brookline, Mass., public library		1
Brooklyn, N. Y., library		2
Brown university, Providence, R. I.		1
Bruce, W. G., Milwaukee	1	
Brymner, D., Ottawa, Canada	1	
Buffalo, N. Y., library		2
" " society of natural sciences	3	6
California, state library, Sacramento, Cal	1	2
" university, Berkeley, Cal		1
Caspar, C. N., Milwaukee	5	88
Chicago, Ill., public library		10
" " theological seminary of the evangelical lutheran church		1
Chicago, Ill., university		1
Chidester, S. W., Milwaukee	10	
Christiania, Norway, Kgl. norske Frederiks universitet		2

Cincinnati, O., public library	1	1
Clark, C. S., Milwaukee	1	
Cleveland, O., public library		1
Coleman, E., Milwaukee	1	
Columbus, O., public library		1
Cook & Son, Thos., New York, N. Y	1	
Cornell university library, Ithaca, N. Y		4
Creighton university, Omaha, Neb		1
Cust, R. N., London, England	1	
Dalton, J. G., Boston, Mass	1	
Denver, Col., public library		2
Detroit, Mich., public library		3
Deuerlich 'sche Buchhandlung, Göttingen, Germany		1
Dotterer, H. S., Philadelphia, Penn	1	
Dover, N. H., public library		1
Drexel institute, Philadelphia, Penn		1
Dziatzko, K., Göttingen, Germany		1
Elizabeth, N. J., public library		1
Ellis, J., M. D., Philadelphia, Penn	1	2
Enoch Pratt free library, Baltimore, Md		2
Eschweiler, C. F., Milwaukee	1	
Fletcher, R., Washington, D. C	1	
Fletcher free library, Burlington, Vt		1
Foote, A. R., Takoma Park, D. C		2
Foster, W. E., Providence, R. I		1
Gauley, M., Detroit, Mich	1	
Germania assembly 2,438 K. O. L., Milwaukee	1	
Gordon, H. L., Chicago, Ill	1	
Gorton & Lidgerwood Co., New York, N. Y		1
Grand Rapids, Mich., public library		1
Green, S. S., Worcester, Mass		1
Hackley public library, Muskegon, Mich	1	
Hamilton, Canada, public library		1
Hardy, G. E., New York, N. Y		1
Hartford, Conn., library association		3
" " theological seminary		1
Harvard university library, Cambridge, Mass		25
Heath & Co., D. C., Boston, Mass	1	
Hickox, J. H., Washington, D. C	28	49
Hiersemann, K. W., Leipzig, Germany	2	

61

Hinton, J. W., Milwaukee......		2
Hoepli, U., Milano, Italy....................	1	
Hooper, S. K., Denver, Col............................	2	
Howard association, London, England..................	1	
Howard memorial library, New Orleans, La..............		1
Illinois, bureau of labor statistics, Springfield, Ill.......	1	
Indiana, bureau of statistics, Indianapolis. Ind...........	1	
Indiana commandery, M. O. L. L. A., Indianapolis, Ind		1
Indiana, state board of health, Indianapolis, Ind........	1	
Indiana, superintendent of public instruction, Indianapolis, Ind...............	1	
James Prendergast free library, Jamestown, N. Y........	1	
Jersey City, N. J., free public library....................	1	5
John Hopkins hospital, Baltimore, Md................ ...	1	
John Hopkins university, Baltimore, Md.		6
Jones, H. C., New York, N. Y............................		1
Kansas City, Mo., public library........................		1
Kansas railroad commissioners, Topeka, Kansas.	1	
Kansas university, Topeka, Kansas.......................		1
Keogh, Hon. E., Milwaukee...............................		1
King, Fowle & Co., Milwaukee	9	
Koeppen, G., Milwaukee.................................	1	
Koopman, H. S., Bulrington, Vt......		1
Lafayette, Ind., public library...........................		3
Lake Forest, Ill., university.............................		1
Lawrence, Mass., public library.........................		2
Leeds, England, public free library.......................		1
Leland Stanford Junior university, Palo Alto, Cal.......		4
Linderfelt, K. A., Milwaukee............................	1	
Liverpool, England, free public library.......		1
Los Angeles, Cal., chamber of commerce.................		1
Los Angeles, Cal., public library........................		5
Lowry, A. E., Milwaukee................................	1	
Lowther, T. D., Chicago, Ill.............................	1	
Lynde, Mrs. W. P., Milwaukee...........	4	1
Lynn, Mass., public library.............................		1
McClurg & Co., A. C., Chicago, Ill......................	1	
Macdonald, A., Washington, D. C......................		1
Maimondes library, New York, N. Y........................		1
Manchester, England, public free libraries.......		1

APPENDIX F.

NEWSPAPERS AND MAGAZINES ON FILE

IN THE GENERAL READING ROOM.

———

AMERICA.

Boston, Mass., Advertiser, D.
  Christian register, W. (Gift of the publishers.)
  Civil service record, Irr. (Gift of the publishers.)
  Literary world, SM.
  New Nation, W.
  Youth's companion, W.
Chicago, Ill., Gamla och nya hemlandet, (*Swedish*), W. (Gift of the
    publishers).
  Graphic, W.
  Illinois Staatszeitung, (*German*), D.
  National zeitung, W.
  Nederlander, De. (Gift of the publishers.)
  Open court, W.
  Skandinaven, (*Norwegian*), D.
  Street railway review, M. (Gift of the publishers.)
  Svenska tribunen, W. (Gift of the publishers.)
  Times, D.
  Tribune, D.
Detroit, Mich., Tageblatt, D. (Gift of the publishers.)
Hartford, Conn., Travelers' record, M. (Gift of the publishers.)
Madison, Wis., Northwestern mail, W. (Gift of the publishers.)
  State journal, D.
  Wisconsin staatszeitung, W. (Gift of the publishers.)
Medford, Wis., Waldbote, (*German*), W. (Gift of the publishers).

Milwaukee, Wis., Abend-post, (*German*), D.

    Amerikanische turnzeitung, (*German*), W.

    Calumet, W.

    Columbia, (*German*), W.

    Domácnost, (*Polish*), W.

    Erziehungs-blätter, (*German*), M.

    Evening Wisconsin, D.

    Excelsior, (*German*), W.

    Freidenker, (*German*), W.

    Germania, (*German*), SW.

    Germania, (*German*), D.

    Haus- und bauernfreund, (*German*), W.

    Herold, (*German*), D.

    Journal, D.

    Kinder-post, (*German*), W.

    Kuryer Polski. (Polish), D.

    News, D.

    Our young people, W.

    Peck's sun, W.

    Proceedings of the common council, BW.

    Proceedings of the school board, M.

    Realty and building record, W.

    Rovnost (*Bohemian*), D.

    Saturday star, W.

    Seebote, (*German*), D.

    Sentinel, D.

    Sunday telegraph, W.

    Telephon (*German*), W.

    United states miller, M.

    Volks-zeitung, (*German*), D.

    Wisconsin weather and crop journal, M.

    Wisconsin times, W.

    Yenowine's Sunday news, W.

    Young churchman, W.

    Zgoda, (*Polish*), W.

New Orleans, La., Picayune, D.

New York, N. Y., American machinist, W.

    Army and navy journal, W.

    Bellestristisches journal, (*German*), W.

    Cook's excursionist, M. (Gift of the publishers.)

Gift of the publishers.

Courier des Etats-Uuis, (*French*), W.

Electrical engineer, W.

Engineering and building record, W.

Epoch, W.

Frank Leslie's illustrated newspaper, W.

Free Russia, M.

Garden and forest, W.

Harpers' weekly, W.

Iron age, W.

Jeweler's weekly, W. (Gift of the publishers.)

Judge, W.

Literary news, M.

Literary world. SM.

Nation, W.

Puck, W.

Science, W.

Scientific american, W.

Scientific american supplement, W.

Staatszeitung, (*German*), D.

Tribune, D.

Turf, field and farm, W.

Voice, W. (Gift of the publishers.)

World, D.

Omaha, Neb.. Bee, D. (Gift of the publishers.)

Pittsburgh, Pa., Christian statesman, W. (Gift of the publishers.)

San Francisco, Cal., Chronicle, D.

Stoughton, Wis., Normannen, (*Swedish*).

Toronto, Ont., Globe, D.

Washington, D. C., Congressional record, D. (Gift).

Public opinion, W.

FRANCE.

Paris. L'illustration, W.

GERMANY.

Berlin, Kladderadatsch, W.

Bremen, Weser zeitung, W.

Cöthen, Chemiker zeitung, W.

Halle, Natur, W.

Köln, Kölnischne zeitung, W.

Leipzig, Gartenlaube, W.

Illustrirte zeitung, W.

Munich, Fliegende blätter, W.

Stuttgart, Ueber land und meer, W.

GREAT BRITAIN AND IRELAND.

Dublin, United Ireland, W.

Glasgow, Herald, W.

London, Academy, W.

Athenæum, W.

British journal of photography, W.

Field, W.

Graphic, W.

Illustrated news, W.

Phonetic journal, W. (Gift.)

Punch, W.

Saturday review, W.

Times, W.

IN THE LADIES' READING ROOM.

(IN ADDITION TO THOSE IN THE GENERAL ROOM.)

Boston, Mass., Woman's journal, W.

Milwaukee, Wis., Evening Wisconsin, D.

Herold, D.

Sentinel, D.

New York, N. Y., Harper's bazar, W.

Harper's weekly, W.

ON APPLICATION AT THE COUNTER IN THE READING ROOM.

AMERICA.

American agriculturist, New York, M.

American anthropologist, Washington, Q.

American antiquarian, Chicago, BM.

American architect and building news, Boston, W.

American chemical journal, Baltimore, B.M

American journal of archæology, Baltimore, Q.

American journal of mathematics. Baltimore, Q.

American journal of philology, Baltimore, Q.

American journal of science, New Haven, M.

American meterological journal, Detroit, M.

American microscopical journal, Washington, M.

American naturalist, Philadelphia, M.

American notes and queries, Philadelphia, W.

American philatelist, M. (Gift.)
Andover review, Boston, M.
Annals of the American academy, Philadelphia, B.M.
Architectural review, Boston, 8 times yearly.
Architecture and building, New York, W.
Arena, Boston, M.
Armer teufel, Der. (Gift.)
Atlantic monthly, Boston, M.
Beacon, New York, M.
Belford's magazine, Chicago, M.
Book news, Phila., M.
Business, New York, M.
California magazine, San Francisco, M.
Carpentry and building, New York, M.
Catholic world, New York, M.
Century magazine, New York, M.
Charities review, New York, M.
Chautauquan, Meadville, Pa., M.
Commonwealth, Chicago, M.
Cosmopolitan, New York, M.
Critic, New York, W.
Current literature, New York, M.
Decorator and furnisher, New York, M.
Dial, Chicago, M.
Eclectic magazine, New York, M.
Education, Boston, M.
Educational review, New York, M.
Engineering magazine, New York, M.
Engineering news, New York, W.
Etude, Philadelphia, M.
Far and near, New York, M.
Forum, New York, M.
Globe, Philadelphia, Q.
Goldthwaites' geographical magazine, New York, M.
Good roads, New York, M.
Harper's monthly, New York, M.
Harper's young people, New York, W.
Insect life, M. (Gift).
International journal of ethics, Philadelphia, Q.
Johns Hopkins University Studies in historical and political science,
    Baltimore, M.

Journal of american folk-lore, Boston, Q.
Journal of comparative medicine, New York, M.
Journal of morphology, Boston, Irr.
Journal of the Franklin institute, Philadelphia, M.
Keynote, New York, M.
Ladies home journal, Philadelphia, M.
Lend a hand, Boston, M.
Lippincott's magazine. Philadelphia, M.
Littell's living age, Boston, W.
Litterarisches echo, Leipzig, M.
Magazine of American History, New York, M.
Magazine of christian literature, New York, M.
Magazine of poetry, Buffalo, Q.
Monist, Chicago, Q.
Mother's nursery guide, New York, M.
Music, Chicago, M. (Gift of the editor).
National magazine, New York, M.
New England historical and genealogical register, Boston, Q.
New England magazine. Boston, M.
New review, New York, M.
North American review, New York, M.
Official gazette of the U. S. patent office, Washington, W. (Gift of the
    Patent office.)
Outing, New York, M.
Overland monthly, San Francisco, M.
Pedagogical seminary, Worcester, Mass., 3 times yearly.
Philosophical review. Boston, Q.
Photo-American review, New York, M.
Photographic times, New York, W. (Gift.)
Poet lore, Boston, M.
Political science quarterly, Boston, Q.
Popular science monthly. New York, M.
Power, New York, M.
Quarterly journal of economics, Boston, Q.
Quarterly register of current history. Detroit, Q.
Queries, Buffalo, M.
Railroad and engineering journal, New York, M.
Review of reviews, New York, M.
St. Nicholas, New York, M.
Sanitarian, New York, M.

Scientific American, architects' and builders' edition. New York, M.
Scribner's magazine, New York, M.
Shakespeariana, New York, Q.
Social economist, New York. M.
Truth-seeker, New York. W. (Gift.)
United Service, Philadelphia, M.
University extension, Philadelphia, M.
Werner's voice magazine, New York, M.
Whist, Milwaukee, M.
Wide awake, Boston, M.

FRANCE.

Revue de famille, Paris, SM.
Revue des deux mondes, Paris, SM.
Revue encyclopédique, Paris, SM.

GERMANY.

Deutsche revue, Berlin, M.
Deutsche rundschau, Berlin, M.
Dingler's polytechnishes journal, Stuttgart. W.
Geographische mittheilungen Gotha, M.
Nord und süd, Breslau. M.
Salon, Leipzig, M.
Unsere zeit, Leipzig, M.
Vom fels zum meer, Stuttgart, M.
Westermann's monatshefte, Brunswick, M.
Zeitschrift für vergleichende litteraturgeschichte, Berlin, Q.

GREAT BRITAIN AND IRELAND.

All the year round, London, W.
Antiquary, London, M.
Argosy, London, M.
Belgravia, London, M.
Blackwood's Edinburgh magazine, Edinburgh, M.
Chambers's journal, Edinburgh, M.
Contemporary review, London, M.
Cornhill magazine, London, M.
Dublin review, Dublin, Q.
Edinburgh review, Edinburgh, Q.
Engineering, London, W.
English historical review, London, Q.
English illustrated magazine, London, M.

73

Fortnightly review, London, M.
Gentleman's magazine, London, M.
Geographical society's proceedings, London, M.
Good words, London, M.
Journal of the Anthropological institute, London, M.
Journal of the Statistical society, London, Q.
Knowledge, London, M.
London society, London, M.
Longman's magazine, London, M.
Macmillan's magazine, London, M.
Mind, London, Q.
Month, London, M.
National review, London, M.
Nature, London, W.
Nineteenth century, London, M.
Notes and queries, London, W.
Observatory, London, M.
Quarterly review, London, Q.
Review of reviews, London, M.
Scottish geographical magazine, Edinburgh, M.
Scottish review, London, Q.
Temple bar, London, M.
Westminster review, London, M.

IN THE REFERENCE ROOM.

Art amateur, New York, M.
Art journal, London, M.
Magazine of art, London, M.
Portfolio, London, M.

IN THE LIBRARIAN'S ROOM.

Allgemeine bibliographie für Deutschland, Leipzig, W.
American bookmaker, M.
Art, L', et l' idée, Paris, M.
Appleton's literary bulletin, New York, M. (Gift of the publishers.)
Author, Boston, M.
Bibliographie de la France, Paris, W.
Book buyer, New York, M.
Book chat, New York, M.
Book prices current, London, M.
Book worm, London, M.
Catalogue mensuel de la librairie francaise, Paris, M.

Centralblatt für bibliothekswesen, Leipzig, M.
Deutsche literaturzeitung, Berlin, W.
Hinrichs' Bücherverzeichniss, Leipzig, Q. and SA.
Illustrated world's fair, Chicago, M.
Johns Hopkins university circulars, Baltimore, M. (Gift of the pubs.)
Library, London, M.
Library journal, New York, M.
Literary light, Minneapolis, M.
Literary news, New York, M.
Literary world, Boston, SM.
Litterarischer merkur, Leipzig, SM.
Publishers' circular, London, SM.
Publishers' weekly, N. Y., W.
Torch and colonial book circular, London, Q.
U. S. government publications monthly catalogue, Wash., M.
World's Columbian exposition, Chicago, M.
Writer, Boston, M.

Explanation of abbreviations used to denote frequency of publication: SD—twice a day; D—daily; W—weekly; SW—twice a week; BW—every two weeks, SM—twice a month; M—monthly; BM—every two months; Q—four times a year; SA—twice a year.

SIXTEENTH

ANNUAL REPORT

OF THE

BOARD OF TRUSTEES

OF THE

PUBLIC LIBRARY

OF THE

CITY OF MILWAUKEE.

OCTOBER 1ST, 1893.

MILWAUKEE.
EDWARD KEOGH, PRINTER.
1893.

LIBRARY SERVICE.

August 31, 1893.

Miss THERESA HUBBELL WEST, Librarian.
SAMUEL R. BELL, Librarian's Clerk.

CATALOGUING DEPARTMENT.

Miss AGNES VAN VALKENBURGH, Cataloguer.

REFERENCE DEPARTMENT.

Miss WILLY SCHMIDT, Reference Librarian and First Assistant.
RUSSELL W. FISH, Evening Assistant (Acting).

ISSUING DEPARTMENT.

Miss LUTIE EUGENIA STEARNS, Superintendent.
Miss BELLE BLEND, Assistant.
Miss KAREN SCHUMACHER, Assistant,
Miss JOSEPHINE BUNTESCHU, Assistant.
Miss EMILY LOUISE CORBITT, Assistant.
Miss ANNA MARION SULLIVAN, Assistant.
EDWARD ALDEN DONALDSON, Evening Attendant.
ROY J. FISH, Saturday Attendant.

READING ROOMS.

Mrs. EVA SHEAFE COE, Superintendent.
Miss AGNES SULLIVAN, Assistant.

JANITOR.

HEINRICH SCHWARTZ.

NIGHT WATCHMAN.

DAVID EDWARD DALE.

REPORT OF THE BOARD OF TRUSTEES.

SEPTEMBER 1st, 1893.

To the Honorable the Common Council of the City of Milwaukee:

GENTLEMEN:—In accordance with the provisions of the law under which the Public Library was established, I have the honor to submit hereby the annual report of the Board of Trustees.

The specific work of the library is detailed in the report of the Librarian to the Board of Trustees, which is appended and which may be consulted to ascertain the growth of the library, both in accumulation of books and in the appreciation of the citizens for whose use it is maintained.

The Board of Trustees, together with the Board of Trustees of the Public Museum, are about to advertise for plans for the joint building, for which your honorable body has so generously provided funds.

It is hoped that another year may show the building, which is so much needed by both institutions, well advanced toward completion.

For the Board of Trustees of the Milwaukee Public Library,

MATTHEW KEENAN,
President.

REPORT OF THE LIBRARIAN.

MILWAUKEE, September 1st, 1893.

To the Board of Trustees of the Milwaukee Public Library:

GENTLEMEN: In conformity to your rules for the government of the library, I have the honor to submit herewith the report of the Librarian and Secretary on the condition and working of the library for the official year ending August 31st, 1893, being the 16th annual report since the organization of the library.

The chief event of the library year is, without doubt, the vote of the Common Council of the city to issue additional Library Museum bonds to the amount of $350,000. This makes it possible to proceed to the final steps for erecting the Library-Museum building on the beautiful site, the purchase of which has been chronicled in previous reports. This sum, with the amount already issued, and now lying in the city treasury, $160,000, gives us a fund of $510,000 with which to build a suitable home for both institutions. The Boards of Trustees whose energy and devotion have brought this long-desired thing to pass, have earned the appreciation and gratitude of the city, which will certainly find more open expression as the walls of the building grow, during the coming year, toward the complete whole.

It is pleasant to note not only a steady but quite a large growth in the use of the library even under the present unfavorable conditions. The changes in the rooms made during July have relieved the crowding of the shelves for the present, but many most attractive possibilities are necessarily left undeveloped until we can have the larger opportunity of the new building. For instance, the possibility of asking teachers to bring their little folk, by classes, to the library and there to show them the books and pictures which are the inviting paths leading out and away beyond the gateways of their school-books and lessons; the possibility of guiding a student to a comfortable seat in a light alcove where the fact in which he is interested is told over and over again, each time with some added light or some further clinch of argument; the possibility of inviting one and another of our fellow-townsmen through the library and showing, in suggestive fashion, not only the treasures already accumulated, but the open space prepared for gifts to help supply the needs of the future; all these and scores of other ideals must wait until the day when the new building is entered and dedicated.

The statistics are, in most cases, from the records of the heads of departments. To the ability and faithfulness of these heads of departments, and their assistants, is justly due much of the credit for the growing usefulness and success of the library. The tabulated statements, which need little verbal comment, follow in the order chosen for former reports.

BOOKS.

On hand Sept. 1, 1892		64,217 vols.
Added. Sept. 1, 1892—August 31, 1893.		
By gift	311 vols.	
By purchase and exchange	4,092 "	
By transfer by binding	379 "	
		4,782 vols.
Total		68,999 vols.
Withdrawn, Sept. 1, 1892—Aug. 31, 1893.		
Books discarded	119 vols.	
Books lost and paid for	17 "	
		136 vols.
In the library Aug. 31, 1893		68,863 vols.

PAMPHLETS.

By gift	600 pams.	
By purchase	8 "	
Total		608 pams.

The number of books bought during the year is smaller than usual. This is due to the fact that for the three months past it has been thought wise to buy no more than was absolutely necessary on account of lack of available money in the city treasury.

CLASSIFICATION OF ACCESSIONS.

	Volumes.	Percentage.
General and bibliographical works	476	9.9
Philosophy and ethics	43	.9
Religion and theology	194	4.1
Social and political science	510	10.7
Philology	26	.5
Natural science	186	3.9
Useful arts	221	4.6
Fine arts	118	2.5
Literature in general	289	6.
Poetry and drama	356	7.4
Prose fiction and children's stories	950	19.9
History	500	10.5
Geography and travels	164	3.4
Biography	749	15.7
	4,782	100.0

LANGUAGE.

Volumes in English	4,342	90.8
Volumes in German	398	8.3
Volumes in French	24	.5
Volumes in other languages	18	.4
	4,782	100.0

BINDING.

Books rebound	1,703
Pamphlets bound	11
New books bound	648
Magazines and newspapers bound	326
Total	2,688

BINDERY ACCOUNT.

DEBIT ACCOUNT.

Cost of machinery and tools	$760 97
Cost of materials	501 28
Cost of wages	1,191 74
Cost of rent	269 32
Cost of fuel	23 00
Total	$2,746 31

CREDIT ACCOUNT.

Value of work produced	$1,752 96
Value of stock on hand	448 10
Value of machinery and tools	760 97
Total	$2,962 03

Showing a balance of $215.72 to the credit of the bindery. It should be added, in justice to the binder, and as data in estimating the success of the experiment, that the prices upon which the value of work produced is computed are low when compared with those put upon similar work at the American Library Association exhibit at the World's Fair. I am satisfied that the work is much superior, more substantial and in better taste, than most of the binding in public libraries.

CIRCULATION OF BOOKS.

In Appendix A will be found the usual detailed statement of the aggregate circulation of the library by months, and in Appendix B the record of the several delivery stations. This table shows that there were 159,613 books taken out for home use during 270.8 working days, a daily average of 589.4.

On July 31st, 1,595 books were issued, the largest number of books ever given out in one day since the founding of the library. The day of smallest circulation in the year, 252, was Sept. 23d. The month of highest daily average of issue was March with an average of 745, and of the lowest, September, with 348.

COMPARATIVE STATEMENT OF CIRCULATION 1890-91—1892-93.

MONTHS.	1890-91.		1891-92.		1892-93.	
	Working days.	Volumes issued.	Working days.	Volumes issued.	Working days.	Volumes issued.
September	25	10,215	25	10,380	11	3,830
October.	26	11,348	27	11,252	25	10,706
November.	23	11,699	24	11,535	24	12,725
December.	24.75	12,960	20	10,764	26	13,769
January.	25.5	17,515	23	13,712	25	17,287
February.	23	14,512	24	15,806	23	16,165
March.	26	15,496	27	16,331	25.8	19,228
April.	25.75	14,076	26	15,693	25	16,730
May	25	11,149	25	14,338	26	14,432
June.	26	18,360	26	16,372	26	16,770
July.	25.25	10,299	25	10,490	7	5,153
August.	26	10,306	13	4,924	27	12,818
Total.	301.25	157,935	285	151,597	270.8	159,613
Daily average. . .	524.3		531.9		589.4	

Through the delivery stations were sent out 14,684 volumes, and through the schools 14,275, while the branch library at Bay View circulated 1,969. The number of books given out at the main library is 142,960, irrespective of the books used within the library rooms, an increase of 10,510 over the year before, although the library was open 15 days less.

CLASSIFICATION OF CIRCULATION.

The percentages of circulation in the different classes of literature, for the last four years, are as follows:

	1889-90.	1890-91.	1891-92.	1892-93.
General works	4.8	4.4	5.1	4.7
Philosophy	.6	.5	.5	.6
Theology	1.1	1.1	1.	1.
Social and political science	1.2	1.2	1.3	1.6
Philology	.1	.1	.1	.1
Natural science	3.2	4.6	4.2	4.8
Useful arts	1.7	1.7	1.9	1.9
Fine arts	1.7	1.8	1.7	1.8
Literature in general	5.2	5.	5.	5.2
Prose fiction	48.2	46.2	47.	47.5
Children's stories	18.9	19.4	18.5	17.7
History	5.3	6.1	5.9	6.1
Geography and travels	5.4	5.3	5.	4.8
Biography	2.6	2.6	2.8	2.2

THE LIBRARY AND THE PUBLIC SCHOOLS.

Books for children in the schools have been sent out in the
same way as in former years. The library force notes with
great pleasure the fact that several teachers express much
appreciation of the benefit and inspiration which comes
through this apparent addition to their labors. Very few
teachers who try the plan ever give it up. One session
of the American Library Association convention in Chicago
this year was given to the discussion of the work done in
this line throughout the country. The conclusion was inev-
itable to my mind that this library is really making the most
systematic effort in this direction of any library reporting.

The presence of the chief officers of the school system in the
Board of Trustees gives us a closer touch with the schools
than would otherwise be probable. For instance, I know of
no other case in which the catalogue of books for young people
has been made a part of the manual of instruction. Special
lists of references on holidays of national character, such as
Independence day, Decoration day, Washington's birthday and

Arbor day, which are celebrated in the schools, have been made to help the teachers. The statistics of school circulation appended do not fairly represent the actual work done, as in several instances the teachers did not keep the tabulated record required.

Four thousand three hundred and fifty-one books were issued fourteen thousand two hundred and seventy-five times by fifty-eight teachers in twenty-six schools.

Outside of the public schools books were sent in the same way to the Klauser Conservatory of Music and to the Colored Men's Club, and for use in connection with various university extension courses.

BOOK BORROWERS AND REGISTRATION.

Total registration Sept. 1, 1892	51,557
Cards issued Sept. 1, 1892, to Aug. 31, 1893	5,896
Total registration Sept. 1, 1893	57,453
Cards expired and cancelled Sept. 1, 1892, to Aug. 31, 1893	46,449
Cards in use	11,004

READING ROOMS.

Detailed statistics of visitors to the reading room are to be found in Appendix C.

There are now kept on file 294 serials, of which 244 are magazines or weekly papers, general and special, and fifty are newspapers. The number of magazines is made up of 164 American, 52 English, 22 German and 6 French publications. The newspapers comprise 24 dailies and 26 weeklies, etc., representing the United States, Canada, Great Britain and Ireland, and Germany. Twenty-nine newspapers and 26 magazines are furnished free of charge, a detailed statement of which will be found in Appendix F.

The whole amount paid for subscriptions during the year has been $1,370.40, which includes $268.32 paid for periodicals furnished during the previous year, leaving the actual cost of subscriptions for this year $1,102.08.

REFERENCE ROOM.

The same difficulty in giving a proportionate prominence to the work of the reference room exists that was noted last year. It can be measured, like any other true educational work, only by the growth of the minds of those ministered to, not by statistics. In this room much of the best co-operation with the various classes for study in the city is done, notably the Ladies' Art and Science Class, the history classes conducted by Mrs. Anna R. Sheldon and the various university extension courses organized last winter.

CATALOGUING.

The cataloguing of the accessions of the past year has been done by Miss Agnes Van Valkenburgh with such assistance as the librarian has been able to give. Four numbers of the Quarterly Index of Additions have been published containing lists of books added since January, 1892. Special reading lists on Municipal government and Electricity have been added to two numbers of these quarterlies. The time is not far distant when more assistance will be necessary in this department that the library may be able to do more than to catalogue the new books bought from month to month.

DELIVERY STATIONS.

The six delivery stations have been maintained throughout the year without change.

ADMINISTRATION.

There are sixteen persons regularly employed in the main library, including the janitor and night watchman. The changes in the force during the year have been the resignation of Miss Mary E. Stillwell as stenographer, and the appointment of Miss Van Valkenburgh, as cataloguer; the resignations of Mr. W. J. Kershaw and of Henry Lehfeldt; and the appointment of Miss Anna M. Sullivan.

The election of librarian occurred at the annual meeting in May, when Miss West was chosen for the regular term.

INSURANCE.

Complaint being made by the insurance companies of the form heretofore in use, a special committee was appointed to examine and report. The committee arranged an agreement with the Board of Underwriters by which a special rate was obtained, on condition that the insurance be kept up to the estimated cost of the library. The following schedule is the insurance taken out under this agreement.

INSURANCE IN FORCE SEPT. 1, 1893.

Ætna Insurance Co., Hartford, Conn	$2,500 00
Albany Fire Insurance Co., Albany, N. Y	1,000 00
Allemannia Fire Insurance Co., Pittsburg, Pa	2,500 00
American Fire Insurance Co., Philadelphia, Pa	2,500 00
Boylston Fire Insurance Co., Boston, Mass	2,500 00
British America Assurance Co., Toronto, Canada	2,500 00
Broadway Insurance Co., New York	1,000 00
Buffalo German Insurance Co., Buffalo, N. Y	2,500 00
Capital Insurance Co., Concord, N. H	2,500 00
Citizens' Insurance Co., Pittsburg, Pa	2,500 00
Columbian Insurance Co., Louisville, Ky	2,500 00
Commerce Insurance Co., Albany, N. Y	1,000 00
Detroit Insurance Co., Detroit, Mich	2,500 00
Eagle Insurance Co., New York	2,000 00
Fire Association Insurance Co., Philadelphia, Pa	2,500 00
Fireman's Fund Insurance Co., San Francisco, Cal	2,500 00
Franklin Insurance Co., Philadelphia, Pa	2,500 00
German Insurance Co., Freeport, Ill	2,500 00
German Insurance Co., Pittsburg, Pa	2,500 00
Glens Falls Insurance Co., Glens Falls, N. Y	1,500 00
Hamburg-Bremen Fire Ins. Co., U. S. Branch, New York	2,500 00
Home Insurance Co., New York	2,500 00
Manufacturers' and Merchants' Ins. Co., Pittsburg, Pa	2,500 00

Michigan Insurance Co., Detroit, Mich.....................	2,500 00
Milwaukee Mechanics' Insurance Co., Milwaukee, Wis....	5,000 00
Newark Fire Insurance Co., Newark, N. J.................	2,500 00
Norwich Union Fire Insurance Society, England..........	2,500 00
Oakland, California.....................................	2,500 00
Palatine, England......................................	2,500 00
Pennsylvania Fire Insurance Co., Philadelphia, Pa........	5,000 00
Phœnix, Brooklyn, N. Y.................................	2,500 00
Rhode Island Underwriters' Association, Providence, R. I..	2,500 00
Rochester German Insurance Co., Rochester, N. Y........	2,500 00
Rockford Insurance Co., Rockford, Ill....................	2,500 00
Royal Insurance Co., Liverpool, England................	2,500 00
St. Paul Fire and Marine Insurance Co., St. Paul, Minn....	1,500 00
Security Insurance Co., New Haven, Conn...............	2,500 00
Sun Fire Office, England...............................	2,500 00
Traders' Insurance Co., Chicago, Ill....................	2,500 00
Transatlantic, Germany................................	2,000 00
Western Assurance Co., Toronto, Canada................	2,500 00
Williamsburgh City Insurance Co., Brooklyn, N. Y........	2,500 00
	$102,500 00
Capital Insurance Co. of Concord, N. H., on Bindery......	$1,000 00

FINANCIAL REPORT.

In conclusion, I beg leave to submit the usual statement of the receipts and expenditures of the library during the year, including both the miscellaneous receipts of the librarian and the account with the city treasurer, as follows:

CASH ACCOUNT.

RECEIPTS.

Balance on hand Sept. 1, 1892........................	$70 77	
Received for fines for undue detention of books.......	423 14	
Received for catalogues, etc., sold.....	58 51	
Received for security deposits.......................	63 00	
Received for books lost or damaged..................	20 70	
Received for lost cards replaced.......	15 60	
		651 72

DISBURSEMENTS.

Paid for security deposits refunded....................	$78	00
Paid for lost books restored..........................	3	85
Paid city treasurer.................................	490	56
Balance on hand Sept. 1, 1893......................	79	31
		———— $651 72

LIBRARY FUND ACCOUNT.

DEBIT.

Balance reported in fund Sept. 1, 1892..........	$8,457.54
Appropriation for 1893.........................$30,982.29	

Deposited by Librarian—

Oct. 5. 1892,	Treas. receipt No.	1,734	$11.19		
Nov. 4. "	"	"	" 1,746	31.75	
Dec. 31. "	"	"	" 1,751	71.57	
Jan. 6. 1893	"	"	" 1,762	56.35	
Feb. 4. "	"	"	" 1,767	48.52	
Mch. 6. "	"	"	" 1,773	44.70	
April 10. "	"	"	" 1,781	44.38	
May. 4. "	"	"	" 1,788	61.00	
June 6. "	"	"	" 1,793	63.84	
July 6. "	"	"	" 1,802	57.26	
				——— $490.56	
				———	$31,472.85
					$39,930.39

CREDIT.

Amount of orders drawn for account of—

Rent.................................$	1,594.49
Salaries..............................	10,525.15
Fuel and gas..........................	1,497.13
Books................................	3,943.12
Newspapers and periodicals..............	1,370.40
Postage and express.....................	56.28
Furniture and repairs....................	579.81
Stationery and printing..................	516.33
Catalogues, etc.........................	299.75
Insurance.............................	1,279.25

Binding.......................................	$2,004.60
Delivery stations............................	911.75
Building.....................................	30.00
Miscellaneous...............................	188.55
	————— $24,796.61

Balance in fund Sept. 1, 1893............. $15,133.78

All of which is respectfully submitted.

THERESA HUBBELL WEST,
Librarian and Secretary.

AGGREGATE CIRCULATION.

	Days open.	General works.	Philosophy.	Theology.	Social and political science.	Philology.	Natural science.	Useful arts.	Fine arts.	Literature.	Prose fiction.	Children's fiction.	History.	Geography.	Biography.	Total circulation.	Date and highest circulation.	Date and lowest circulation.	Daily average.	Number of cards issued.	Notices sent.
September, 1882	11	186	41	38	65	7	259	86	62	179	1,753	618	210	187	187	3,890	20-494	29-252	348	288	42
October, "	25	487	69	103	178	13	381	188	202	550	5,514	1,612	619	466	324	10,706	22-785	31-255	428	665	197
November, "	24	653	80	160	235	14	596	200	249	755	6,419	1,850	665	502	347	12,725	28-769	11-354	580	882	315
December, "	26	927	104	158	218	12	642	206	210	789	6,693	2,200	784	555	351	13,769	3-895	18-350	580	490	262
January, 1883	25	785	92	140	265	26	834	225	317	1,027	7,357	3,172	1,154	1,028	565	17,287	21-898	10-396	691	790	313
February, "	23	800	85	201	307	18	635	305	326	869	7,468	3,199	870	859	560	16,165	11-485	3-387	703	718	274
March, "	25.8	844	83	169	362	22	1,250	379	357	1,063	8,561	3,383	1,272	1,039	618	19,228	4-1076	22-355	745	705	286
April, "	25	821	100	158	284	19	933	283	263	814	7,410	2,636	1,034	825	492	16,730	8-992	26-300	689	403	392
May, "	26	608	138	130	280	24	640	283	263	710	7,281	3,065	687	554	440	14,432	18-890	10-395	555	385	370
June, "	28	675	42	100	169	12	1,209	292	233	833	6,433	3,088	1,218	1,160	429	16,770	3-690	20-321	645	308	443
July, "	7	192	32	45	51	10	124	88	84	187	2,999	688	174	138	93	5,153	31-1566	7-514	738	97	90
August, "	27	541	74	110	158	12	307	286	281	500	7,256	2,372	413	308	190	12,818	14-682	4-281	475	485	800
Total	270.8	7,519	988	1,510	2,572	189	7,710	8,001	2,807	8,246	75,776	28,217	8,960	7,622	4,546	159,613	1566	252	589.4	5,896	8,284
Per cent		4.7	.6	1.	1.6	.1	4.8	1.9	1.8	5.2	47.5	17.7	6.1	4.8	2.2	100					

APPENDIX B.

CIRCULATION OF DELIVERY STATIONS.

A.—SOUTH SIDE, FIRST AVENUE.

	Days open.	General works.	Philosophy.	Theology.	Social and political science.	Philology.	Natural science.	Useful arts.	Fine arts.	Literature.	Prose fiction.	Children's fiction.	History.	Geography.	Biography.	Total circulation.	Date and highest circulation.	Date and lowest circulation.	Daily average.
September, 1892	10			1	2		7	2	1	9	64	32	8	8	9	141	21—57	22—0	14
October, 1892	25	16	1		2		7	7	7	11	126	70	31	7	4	289	10—31	31—3	12
November, 1892	24	15	2		3		20	4	4	14	136	92	27	6	2	324	10—31	7—4	13
December, 1892	26	11	2	1	3		13	12	8	16	130	112	29	5	4	346	1—29	12—2	13
January, 1893	25	25		1	3		10	7	5	3	169	111	13	8	3	358	4—29	9—2	15
February, 1893	23	21		1	4		7	4	12	8	175	106	21	20	5	383	17—33	20—3	17
March, 1893	24	19	1				17	11	1	11	163	119	37	18	5	402	2—43	27—7	17
April, 1893	25	13	2	2	3		14	12	3	8	132	111	17	15	5	340	25—22	10—3	14
May, 1893	26	30	2	1	2		17	4	3	8	135	133	27	14	7	384	3—26	23—6	15
June, 1893	26	23	1	1	1		11	5	3	8	166	165	30	8	3	426	1—33	19—8	16
July, 1893	7	6	1	1	1		1	5	3		84	70	5	8		185	31—98	8—5	26
August, 1893	27	11	1				5	6	2	7	147	100	10	7	5	302	1—23	5—1	11
Total	268	192	13	9	24		129	79	52	103	1627	1221	255	124	52	3880	98	0	14.4
Per cent		5.	.3	.2	.6		3.3	2.	1.3	2.7	42.	31.5	6.6	3.2	1.3				

APPENDIX B.—Continued.
CIRCULATION OF DELIVERY STATIONS.

B.—EAST SIDE.

	Days open	General works	Philosophy	Theology	Social and political science	Philology	Natural science	Useful arts	Fine arts	Literature	Prose fiction	Children's fiction	History	Geography	Biography	Total circulation	Date and highest circulation	Date and lowest circulation	Daily average
September, 1892	10	..	1	1	3	..	4	1	..	5	57	12	6	1	4	95	20—37	26—0	10
October, 1892	25	7	5	..	..	..	8	1	..	6	126	21	12	3	2	191	6—20	3—1	8
November, 1892	24	7	5	2	1	..	..	2	3	11	101	27	8	7	1	175	10—17	22—2	7
December, 1892	26	6	..	..	2	..	5	2	3	10	90	30	11	..	..	159	13—14	12—1	6
January, 1893	25	5	..	..	3	..	1	..	3	9	112	35	10	7	9	195	4—29	9—2	8
February, 1893	23	11	1	2	1	..	2	1	2	13	105	34	9	6	1	185	7—23	27—2	8
March, 1893	24	13	4	1	4	..	5	2	1	8	143	38	13	1	5	240	6—24	16—4	10
April, 1893	25	11	3	3	1	..	8	..	2	6	158	45	9	3	5	254	11—18	17—5	10
May, 1893	26	8	2	1	..	..	9	..	..	7	170	48	8	8	3	265	4—16	29—5	10
June, 1893	7	1	1	2	2	..	1	..	1	8	203	49	3	5	3	294	21—27	23—4	11
July, 1893	..	1	1	..	3	1	1	..	..	..	102	14	2	1	..	137	31—63	8—6	20
August, 1893	27	9	2	..	..	..	1	..	1	5	170	53	1	9	3	269	12—20	7—2	..
Total	268	85	34	13	21	1	52	11	16	88	1,537	406	102	57	36	2,459	63	0	9.2
Per cent	..	3.5	1.4	.5	.9	.1	2.1	.4	.7	3.6	62.5	16.5	4.	2.3	1.5	..	..	..	..

APPENDIX B—Continued.

CIRCULATION OF DELIVERY STATIONS.

C.—THIRD STREET.

	Days open.	General works.	Philosophy.	Theology.	Social and political science.	Philology.	Natural science.	Useful arts.	Fine arts.	Literature.	Prose fiction.	Children's fiction.	History.	Geography.	Biography.	Total circulation.	Date and highest circulation.	Date and lowest circulation.	Daily average.
September, 1892	10	6		1	2		6	3	3	4	41	27	12	1	4	107	20—58	24—1	11
October, "	25	12			5		10	3	1	4	66	46	19	10	1	175	24—23	3—1	7
November, "	24	25	1		3		9	5	3	10	73	74	20	7	3	235	19—19	25—4	10
December, "	26	23		1	3		21	8	1	11	75	60	64	6	3	275	23—20	19—5	11
January, 1893	25	21	1	2	3		16	4	5	7	100	61	27	11	4	260	25—21	23—3	10
February, "	23	20	1	5	2		13	5	8	9	95	83	24	16	4	282	1—21	6—5	12
March, "	24	28		2	3		10	8	8	17	123	112	37	12	1	360	2—34	14—5	15
April, "	25	25			4		14	9	4	6	89	108	27	15	3	306	11—22	17—6	12
May, "	26	30		3	3		18	11	6	15	115	136	37	13	6	390	18—26	19—5	15
June, "	26	31		1	7		21	2	5	11	115	204	26	16	3	444	1—31	17—5	17
July, "	7	11			1		2	2		3	66	77	12	11		186	31—95	5—6	27
August, "	27	24			6		6		1	5	125	146	24	15	2	354	30—43	25—2	13
Total	268	251	3	15	39		146	60	45	102	1083	1134	329	133	34	3374	95		12.6
Per cent		7.4	.1	.4	1.2		4.3	1.8	1.3	3.	32.1	33.6	9.8	3.9	1.1				

APPENDIX B.—CONTINUED.

CIRCULATION OF DELIVERY STATIONS.

D.—WALNUT STREET.

	Days open	General works	Philosophy	Theology	Social and political science	Philology	Natural science	Useful arts	Fine arts	Literature	Prose fiction	Children's fiction	History	Geography	Biography	Total circulation	Date and highest circulation	Date and lowest circulation	Daily average
September, 1892	10	3				1	4			2	37	17	3		4	72	21—27	22—0	7
October, "	25	9		1	1		1	2		6	81	41	15	3	5	164	6—24	14—2	7
November, "	24	13		1	1		1	1	2	8	73	42	12	4	5	163	17—18	1—2	6
December, "	26	10			1		4	3		8	75	25	26	2	1	150	17—17	31—2	7
January, 1893	25	11	1	2	1		2	2	2	2	87	36	17	4	4	176	21—20	11—2	8
February, "	23	15		1	2		1	4	2	12	98	40	11	3	2	188	7—22	15—2	9
March, "	24	12	1	1	1		1	2	1	13	98	56	9	6	1	204	7—19	29—3	8
April, "	25	8		3	2		2		1	15	107	51	9	8		199	18—20	28—2	8
May, "	26	1	1		1		5	1	1	3	116	50	5	3	2	196	9—17	8—2	9
June, "	26	2		3	1		3	1	1	3	116	81	5	2	1	228	22—22	17—2	22
July, "	7	4		2			5	3	3	2	55	62	11	4		152	31—84	3—5	9
August, "	27	14		1	2		5	5	6	7	99	79	10	3	3	232	29—28	7—1	9
Total	268	121	2	14	12	1	34	24	17	68	1,042	580	133	42	34	2,124	84	0	7.9
Per cent.		5.7	.1	.7	.6	.1	1.6	1.1	.8	3.2	49.1	27.3	6.2	1.9	1.6				

APPENDIX B.—Continued.

CIRCULATION OF DELIVERY STATIONS.

E.—BAY VIEW.

	Days open.	General works.	Philosophy.	Theology.	Social and political cal science.	Philology.	Natural science.	Useful arts.	Fine arts.	Literature.	Prose fiction.	Children's fiction.	History.	Geography.	Biography.	Total circulation.	Date and highest circulation.	Date and lowest circulation.	Daily average.
September, 1892	10	1	1								34	4				39	20–11	23–0	4
October, 1892	25	1	1	1	1		2		2		60	10	8	1	2	81	19–8	3–1	3
November, 1892	24				2		1	3		3	74	13	8	2		104	19–9	14–0	4
December, 1892	26	3	1				1	1		1	82	16	5	1		112	17–9	22–1	5
January, 1893	25	1	3	1	3		2		1	2	85	21	8	2	3	121	24–11	9–0	4
February, 1893	23	2	1				1	1	1		69	11	1	1	5	92	11–8	16–0	4
March, 1893	24	4	1	1			1	1	1	1	77	16	1		2	99	2–9	13–0	4
April, 1893	25	1	2		3						72	16	5			102	18–10	28–1	4
May, 1893	26		2				1				73	12	1	1	3	101	3–9	4–0	4
June, 1893	26		1		1		2	1			77	8	1			95	23–9	19–1	4
July, 1893	7	3			2		2				27	5	3		1	38	31–24	8–0	5
August, 1893	27										68	29				105	25–15	10–0	4
Total	268	14	9	2	9		11	6	3	3	800	161	42	8	13	1,089	24	0	
Per cent		1.3	.8	.2	.8		1.	.6	.3	.3	73.5	14.8	3.8	.7	1.2				4.1

APPENDIX B.—Continued.

CIRCULATION OF DELIVERY STATIONS.

G.—SOUTH SIDE, GROVE STREET.

	Days open.	General works.	Philosophy.	Theology.	Social and political science.	Philology.	Natural science.	Useful arts.	Fine arts.	Literature.	Prose fiction.	Children's fiction.	History.	Geography.	Biography.	Total circulation.	Date and highest circulation.	Date and lowest circulation.	Daily average.
September, 1892	10	2	1				6	3	4	1	49	15	5	4	4	88	21—47	23—0	9
October, "	25	6						3		2	67	29	15		7	135	7—10	3—1	5
November, "	24	13	1		2		6	6	4	2	76	32	10	8	4	161	29—14	9—1	7
December, "	26	4		2	3		10	5	3	2	67	21	10	2		126	8—9	17—1	5
January, 1893	25	10	1	1	5		7	7	1	2	84	33	11	3		164	30—11	14—2	7
February, "	23	6			2		4	5		3	84	34	17	8		167	24—17	27—3	7
March, "	24	10			4		4	2	1	2	99	46	8	5	1	179	6—22	9—3	7
April, "	25	11	1	1	1		3	3	2	6	80	38	9	10	2	168	20—13	17—4	7
May, "	26	24			1		3	3	1	4	93	64	6	4		206	26—12	16—3	8
June, "	26	12					1	1	3	1	70	74	15	3	2	184	10—16	27—3	7
July, "	7	1						2	2	1	29	17	7	5		67	31—41	3—1	10
August, "	27	3			1		4	3	3	2	53	37	7			113	16—17	3—1	4
Total	268	102	3	4	19		52	43	24	28	851	440	120	52	20	1758	47	0	6.6
Per cent		5.8	.2	.2	1.1		3.	2.4	1.4	1.6	48.4	25.	6.8	3.	1.1				

APPENDIX B.—CONTINUED.

CIRCULATION OF BAY VIEW BRANCH LIBRARY.

	Days open.	General works.	Philosophy.	Theology.	Social and political science.	Philology.	Natural science.	Useful arts.	Fine arts.	Literature.	Prose fiction.	Children's fiction.	History.	Geography.	Biography.	Total circulation.	Date and highest circulation.	Date and lowest circulation.	Daily average.
September, 1892	11								1	3	37	1			1	42	19— 7	20—0	4
October, "	25									7	91	8	1	2	3	113	17— 9	7—1	5
November, "	24			1						8	110	13	2	4	2	139	28—11	14—1	6
December, "	26			1	1					7	138	16	9	1		171	31—12	2—3	7
January, 1893	25			1						13	128	20	9		2	176	23—13	26—2	7
February, "	23									15	138	27	9	3	3	194	25—18	16—2	8
March, "	24									11	166	48	14		2	248	27—21	8—3	10
April, "	25									13	104	46	13	6	5	183	19—19	3—0	7
May, "	26									20	102	37	8	2		167	13—13	22—0	6
June, "	26									14	96	35	12		3	161	10—16	17—3	6
July, "	7									8	121	32	6	1	6	173	31—13	7—2	25
August, "	27									13	116	55	15	2	1	202	9—10	2—4	7
Total	269			3	1				1	132	1,347	338	98	21	28	1,969	132	0	
Per cent				.1	.1				.1	6.6	68.4	17.2	4.9	1.1	1.4				7.3

APPENDIX B.—CONTINUED.

CIRCULATION THROUGH SCHOOLS.

	General works	Philosophy	Theology	Social and political science	Philology	Natural science	Useful arts	Fine arts	Literature	Prose fiction	Children's fiction	History	Geography	Travel	Total circulation
September, 1892															
October, "															
November, "															
December, "	27			1	2	168	11		8	6	296	55	89	23	686
January, 1893	90	5	8	2		309	37	40	170		963	177	360	39	2206
February, "	62		6	12		167	15	1	16	3	148	127	244	52	844
March, "	102		12	2		691	34	14	171	24	645	369	382	63	2486
April, "	220		8			364	7	20	66	4	1133	196	206	57	2303
May, "	20		3	5	1	122	2	6	11	25	261	64	83		573
June, "	175					849	96	61	200		1910	813	858	181	5177
July, "															
August, "															
Total	696	5	37	22	3	2670	202	142	642	62	5356	1801	2222	415	14275
Per cent	4.8	.1	.3	.2	.1	18.7	1.4	.9	4.5	.4	37.5	12.6	15.6	2.9	

APPENDIX C.

READING ROOM.

	DAYS OPEN.		READERS.			MAGAZINES.			DAILY AVERAGE.			
									READERS.		MAGAZINES.	
	Sec. days.	Sun- days.	Sec. days.	Sun- days.	Total.	Sec. days.	Sun- days.	Total.	Sec. days.	Sun- days.	Sec. days.	Sun- days.
September, 1892	24.5	4	4,336	377	4,713	287	46	333	177	94	12	12
October, "	25	5	3,908	446	4,354	344	53	397	156	89	14	11
November, "	24	4	3,896	423	4,319	369	62	431	162	106	15	16
December, "	26	4	5,518	460	5,978	433	57	490	212	115	17	14
January, 1893	25	5	5,702	517	6,219	523	63	586	228	103	21	13
February, "	23	4	5,344	545	5,889	525	81	606	232	136	23	20
March, "	25.8	5	5,855	727	6,582	582	66	648	227	182	23	17
April, "	25	4	5,110	530	5,640	540	89	629	204	106	14	18
May, "	26	4	4,860	361	5,221	411	55	466	186	90	16	14
June, "	26	4	5,363	297	5,660	404	38	442	206	74	19	10
July, "	7	2	1,577	101	1,678	132	19	151	225	51	17	10
August, "	27	4	6,153	696	6,849	463	43	506	228	174	17	11
Total	284.3	49	57,622	5,480	63,102	5,013	672	5,685	203	112	18	14

APPENDIX D.

COMPARATIVE SUMMARY OF STATISTICS.

	1890–91.	1891–92.	1892–93.
Books in library, beginning of year.........................	52,786	58,959	64,217
Total accessions..............	6,547	5,803	4,782
Given.......................	676	455	311
Transferred by binding.......	474	539	379
Purchased.	5,397	4,809	4,092
Cost of books actually received	$8,745 15	$8,035 69	$3,943 12
Worn out and discarded	354	526	119
Lost, sold and exchanged.....	20	19	17
Pamphlets, accessions	486	541	608
Registered book borrowers, beginning of year..............	41,278	46,449	51,557
New names registered........	5,171	5,108	5,896
Circulation of books............	157,935	151,597	159,613
Working days................	301.25	285	270.8
Daily average................	524.2	531.9	589.4
Largest issue in one day......	950	1,690	1,595
Smallest issue in one day.....	239	274	252
Number of books fined.......	2,272	3,140	3,284
Received for fines............	$457 80	$453 72	$423 14
Reading room—Magazines on file	214	232	242
Newspapers on file..........	56	59	50
Visitors....................	51,049	61,702	63,102
Days open...................	301.25	300	284.3
Average daily attendance.....	169	206	203
Magazines delivered..........	4,031	5,052	5,685
Sunday readers...............	5,859	5,380	5,480
Sundays open...............	52	50	49
Average attendance on Sundays	113	108	112
Magazines delivered..........	716	715	672
Cost of serials...............	$1,026 63	$1,217 27	$1,370 40
Binding and repairing—number volumes.....................	2,682	3,705	2,688
Cost of binding and repairing.	$1,319 40	$4,283 63	$2,004 60
Appropriation, 1891, 1892, 1893..	$28,345 72	$28,418 78	$30,982 29
Amount paid for salaries	$9,037 62	$9,489 97	$10,525 15

The reports for binding for 1890–91 and 1891–92 are divided between the two binderies, that for 1891–92 including the three months' work by our own bindery before the beginning of this report.

APPENDIX—E.

1892-93.

LIST OF GIFTS TO THE LIBRARY.

	Volumes.	Pamphlets.
Aberdeen, Scotland, public library		2
Adams, C. K. Madison, Wisconsin		1
Aguilar free library, New York, N. Y.		2
American academy of the dramatic arts, New York, N. Y.		1
American historical association, Washington, D. C.		1
Amherst, Mass., college		1
Arizona magazine Co., Yuma, Arizona		1
Armour institute, Chicago, Ill		2
Art gravure and etching Co., Milwaukee	1	
Birch's Sons, T:, Philadelphia, Pa	1	4
Birmingham, England, free libraries		1
Bolton, Mrs. S. K., Cleveland, O.		1
Boston children's aid society		1
Boston ladies' commission on Sunday-school books		1
Boston museum of fine arts		1
Boston public library		4
Bowdoin college, Brunswick, Me		1
Bradley, Mrs. W. H., Milwaukee		16
Brett, W. H., Cleveland, O		1
British royal commission for the Chicago exhibition, London, England	1	
Bronson library, Waterbury, Conn		2
Brookline, Mass., public library		1
Brooklyn, N. Y., library		1
Buffalo, N. Y. library		1
California bureau of labor statistics, Sacramento, Cal.		1
California state library, Sacramento, Cal	1	1
California state university, Berkeley, Cal		1
Canada, Dep't of agriculture, archives branch, Ottawa, Canada		1

31

	Volumes.	Pamphlets.
Canada, Royal society of, Montreal, Canada..........	1	
Carnegie free library, Allegheny, Pa............... .		3
Carson Harper Co., Denver Col.....................		2
Caspar, C. N., Milwaukee...........................	10	55
Chatfield & Woods Co., Cincinnati, O.....	1	
Chicago board of education....... ·...............		1
Chicago dep't of public works.......................	1	
Chicago theological seminary of the evangelical lutheran church.................................		1
Chicago, University of..............................		1
Cincinnati, O., public library......................		4
Clarke & Co., R.; Cincinnati, O.....................		1
Cole, T. L., Washington, D. C......................		1
Cornell university, Ithaca, N. Y.......		3
Curtis, G. W., New York, N. Y.....................		1
Cust, R. N., London, England......................	1	1
Dayton, O., public library..........................		1
Denver, Col., Mercantile library....................		1
Detroit, Mich., museum of art......................		1
Detroit, Mich., public library......................		3
Deurlich'sche Buchhandlung, Göttingen, Germany...		5
Doughty, F. W., Brooklyn, N. Y................	1	
Dover, N. H., public library........................		1
Eastburn, G., New York, N. Y......................		2
Ehrenfechter, C. A., London, England..............	1	
Elliott, E. S., Milwaukee...........................	1	
Engholm, E. W., Norrköping, Sweden............,....		1
Enoch Pratt free library, Baltimore, Md.............		2
Fletcher free library, Burlington, Vt................		1
Frick, Rev. W. K., Milwaukee		1
Gammon theological seminary, Atlanta, Georgia.....		1
Germania Publishing Co., Milwaukee...............		1
Gloversville, N. Y., free library...........		1
Grand Rapids, Mich., public school library..........	1	1
Grassie, T: G., Milwaukee.........................		1
Gregory, Maj. James F., Milwaukee.................	2	
Hall & Co., New York, N. Y......................	13	
Hamilton, Canada, public library..................		1
Handsworth, England, public library...............		1
Hartford, Conn., library association................		2

	Volumes.	Pamphlets.
Harvard University, Cambridge, Mass.	1	2
Hoepli, U., Milan, Italy	1	
Howard memorial library, New Orleans, La		1
Illinois state dental society, Chicago, Ill		1
Indian rights association, Philadelphia, Pa		6
Indiana bureau of statistics, Indianapolis, Ind	1	
Indiana state board of health, Indianapolis, Ind	1	
Indianapolis, Ind., public library		1
Iowa, Grand lodge of, Cedar Rapids, Ia	1	
James Prendergast free library, Jamestown, N. Y.		1
Jersey City, N. J., free public library		3
Johns Hopkins university, Baltimore, Md		7
Jones, Prof. G: W., Ithaca, N. Y.	1	
Kansas City, Mo., public library		1
Kansas railroad commissioners, Topeka, Kansas	1	
Lawrence, Mass., public library		2
Leeds, England, public free library		1
Leland Stanford Junior university, Palo Alto, Cal	1	2
Libbie, C. F., & Co., Boston, Mass	.	1
Liverpool, England, free public library		1
Lorck, C. B., Chicago, Ill		1
Los Angeles, Cal., public library		2
Lynn, Mass., public library		1
McGill, P., Milwaukee		1
Macmillan & Co., New York, N. Y		1
Maimonides library, New York, N. Y	.	1
Manchester, England, public free libraries		2
Mapel, J. J., Milwaukee		2
Massachusetts bureau of labor statistics, Boston, Mass..	2	
Massachusetts institute of technology, Boston, Mass..		1
Massachusetts state library, Boston, Mass	1	
Mexican central railway co	1	
Michigan bureau of labor statistics, Lansing, Mich...	1	
Michigan, University of, Ann Arbor, Mich		3
Miller, B. K., Jr., Milwaukee	5	
Mills, S., Madison, Wis	1	
Milwaukee association for the advancement of Mil- waukee	1	
Milwaukee chamber of commerce	1	
Milwaukee commissioner of health		2

	Volumes.	Pamphlets.
Milwaukee county hospital........................		1
Milwaukee mission kindergarten....		1
Milwaukee public museum....		2
Milwaukee real estate board........................	2	
Milwaukee school board...........................		1
Milwaukee seebote................................		1
Minneapolis, Minn., public library..................	1	5
Mitchell, Hon. J. L., Milwaukee...................	3	80
Mitchell library, Glasgow, Scotland.................		1
Morse, E. S., Salem, Mass.........		3
National conference of charities and correction, Boston, Mass.......................................	1	
New Bedford, Mass., board of trade.................	1	
New Bedford, Mass., free public library.............	1	1
New Hampshire state library, Concord, N. H........	7	3
New Haven, Conn.. free public library..............		1
New Jersey bureau of statistics, Trenton, N. J........	1	
New Jersey state library, Trenton, N. J..............	3	
Newark, N. J., free public library..................		2
Newton, Mass., free library........................		1
New York board of women managers, Albany, N. Y..		1
New York, N. Y., free circulating library............	5	2
New York, N. Y., general society of mechanics and tradesmen....................		3
New York, N. Y., mercantile library association......		4
New York, N. Y., school of social economics........		1
New York, N. Y., young men's christian association..		1
New York state library, Albany, N. Y..............		1
New York state university, Albany, N. Y.............		3
Northwestern university, Evanston, Ill..............		1
Oates, W. C., M. C., Washington, D. C..............		3
Oberlin, O., college library........................		1
Ohio historical and philosophical society, Cincinnati, Ohio..................	1	
Ohio state board of agriculture, Columbus, O........		1
Ohio state library, Columbus, O....................		1
Olin, C. C., Indianapolis, Ind......................		1
Omaha, Neb., public library........................		2
Osterhout free library, Wilkes-Barré, Pa.............		2
Paterson, N. J., free public library..................		1

34

	Volumes.	Pamphlets.
Tomlinson, F., Council Bluffs, Iowa		1
Toner, J. M., M. D., Washington, D. C	1	
Toronto, Canada, public library		1
Toronto, Canada, university		1
United States bureau of education	2	6
United States bureau of statistics		8
United States coast and geodetic survey		1
United States commissioner of fish and fisheries	2	
United States commissioner of labor	2	
United States dept. of agriculture	4	76
United States interior dep't	117	29
United States interstate commerce commission	4	
United States navy dep't	1	1
United States patent office	1	
United States state dep't	9	15
United States surgeon-general's office	1	
United States treasury dep't		1
United States war dep't	15	
Unknown	6	4
Upsala, Sweden, universitets-biblioteket		1
Vermont, University of, Burlington, Vt	1	
Victoria university, Toronto, Canada	1	
Ward, C. J. Kingston, Jamaica	1	
Warren county library, Monmouth, Ill		2
Waterhouse, S., St. Louis, Mo	1	9
Watertown, Mass., free public library		1
Welsh, H., New York, N. Y		2
Wisconsin commissioner of labor	1	
Wisconsin commissioner of fisheries		1
Wisconsin grand lodge, I. O. O. F	2	
Wisconsin state board of control of reformatory insti-tions		1
Wisconsin state board of health	1	
Wisconsin state historical society	2	5
Wisconsin state superintendent of public property	12	5
Wisconsin state treasurer	1	
Wisconsin state university		30
Woburn, Mass., public library		1
Worcester, Mass., free public library		1

	Volumes.	Pamphlets.
World's congress auxiliary of the World's Columbian exposition..		2
Wright, A. G., Milwaukee...........................	1	
Yale university, New Haven, Conn..................		4
	311	600

APPENDIX—F.

NEWSPAPERS AND MAGAZINES ON FILE.

IN THE GENERAL READING ROOM.

AMERICA.

Boston, Mass., Advertiser, D.
    Beacon, W.
    Christian register, W. (Gift of the publishers.)
    Literary world, SM.
    New Nation, W.
    Youth's companion, W.
Chicago, Ill., Graphic, W.
    Illinois Staatszeitung, (*German*), D.
    National zeitung, W.
    Nederlander, De. (Gift of the publishers.)
    Open court, W.
    Skandinaven, (*Norwegian*), D.
    Street railway review, M. (Gift of the publishers.)
    Times, D.
    Tribune, D.
Hartford, Conn., Travelers' record, M. (Gift of the publishers.)
Madison, Wis., Northwestern mail, W. (Gift of the publishers.)
    State journal, D.
    Wisconsin Staatszeitung, W. (Gift of the publishers.)
Medford, Wis., Waldbote, (*German*), W. (Gift of the publishers.)

Milwaukee, Wis., Abend-post, (*German*), D.
  Amerikanische turnzeitung, (*German*), W.
  Columbia, (*German*), W.
  Erziehungs-blätter, (*German*), M.
  Evening Wisconsin, D.
  Excelsior (*German*), W.
  Freidenker, (*German*), W.
  Germania, (*German*), SW.
  Germania, (*German*), D.
  Herold, (*German*), D.
  Journal, D.
  Kinder-post, (*German*), W.
  Kuryer Polski, (*Polish*), D.
  Milwaukee record, W.
  News, D.
  Our young people, W.
  Peck's sun, W.
  Proceedings of the common council, BW.
  Proceedings of the school board, M.
  Rovnost, (*Bohemian*), D.
  Saturday star, W.
  Seebote, (*German*), D.
  Sentinel, D.
  Sunday telegraph, W.
  United states miller, M.
  Volks-zeitung, (*German*), D.
  Wisconsin weather and crop journal, M.
  Young churchman, W.
  Zgoda, (*Polish*), W.
New Orleans, La., Picayune, D.
New York, N. Y., American machinist, W.
  Army and navy journal, W.
  Cook's excursionist, M. (Gift of the publishers.)
  Courier des Etats-Unis, (*French*), W.
  Electrical engineer, W.
  Engineering and building record, W.
  Evening post, SW.
  Frank Leslie's illustrated newspaper, W.
  Free Russia, M.
  Garden and forest, W.
  Harper's weekly, W.

Iron age, W.

Jeweler's weekly, W.   (Gift of the publishers.)

Judge, W.

Literary news, M.

Literary world, SM.

Nation, W.

New Yorker volkszeitung, D.

Puck, W.

Science, W.

Scientific american, W.

Scientific american supplement, W.

Staatszeitung, (*German*), D.

Tribune, D.

Tribune, W.   (Gift of the publishers.)

Turf, field and farm, W.

World, D.

Omaha, Neb., Bee, D.   (Gift of the publishers.)

Pittsburgh, Pa., Christian statesman, W.   (Gift of the publishers.)

San Francisco, Cal., Chronicle, D.

Stoughton, Wis., Normannen, (*Swedish*).   (Gift of the publishers.)

Toronto, Ont., Globe, D.

Washington, D. C., Congressional record, D.   (Gift.)

Public Opinion, W.

FRANCE.

Paris, L'illustration, W.

GERMANY.

Berlin, Kladderadatsch, W.

Bremen, Weser zeitung, W.

Cöthen, Chemiker zeitung, W.

Halle, Natur, W.

Köln, Kölnische zeitung, W.

Leipzig, Gartenlaube, W.

Illustrirte zeitung, W.

Munich, Fliegende blätter, W.

Stuttgart, Ueber land und meer, W.

GREAT BRITAIN AND IRELAND.

Dublin, United Ireland, W.

Glasgow, Herald, W.

London, Academy, W.

Athenæum, W.

British journal of photography, W.
Field, W.
Graphic, W.
Illustrated news, W.
Phonetic journal, W.   (Gift.)
Punch, W.
Saturday review, W.
Times, W.

IN THE LADIES' READING ROOM.

(IN ADDITION TO THOSE IN THE GENERAL ROOM.)

Boston, Mass., Woman's journal, W.
Milwaukee, Wis., Evening Wisconsin, D.
     Herold, D.
     Sentinel, D.
New York, N. Y., Harper's bazar, W.
     Harper's weekly, W.

ON APPLICATION AT THE COUNTER IN THE READING ROOM.

AMERICA.

American agriculturist, New York, M.
American anthropologist, Washington, Q.
American antiquarian, Chicago, BM.
American architect and building news, Boston, W.
American chemical journal, Baltimore, BM.
American journal of mathematics, Baltimore, Q.
American journal of philology, Baltimore, Q.
American journal of science, New Haven, M.
American meterological journal, Detroit, M.
American microscopical journal, Washington, M.
American naturalist, Philadelphia, M.
American philatelist, M.   (Gift.)
American school board journal, Milwaukee, M.   (Gift.)
Andover review, Boston, M.
Annals of the American academy, Philadelphia, BM.
Architecture and building, New York, W.
Arena, Boston, M.
Armer teufel, Der, W.   (Gift.)
Atlantic monthly, Boston, M.
Belford's magazine, Chicago, M.

Bohemian voice, Omaha, M. (Gift.)

Book news, Phila., M.

Business, New York, M.

California magazine, San Francisco, M.

Carpentry and building, New York, M.

Catholic world, New York, M.

Century magazine, New York, M.

Charities review, New York, M.

Chautauquan, Meadville, Pa., M.

Cosmopolitan, New York, M.

Critic, New York, W.

Current literature, New York, M.

Decorator and furnisher, New York, M.

Dial, Chicago, M.

Eclectic magazine, New York, M.

Education, Boston, M.

Educational review, New York, M.

Employer and employed, Boston, Q.

Engineering magazine, New York, M.

Engineering news, New York, W.

Etude, Philadelphia, M.

Far and near, New York, M.

Forum, New York, M.

Globe, Philadelphia, Q.

Goldthwaites' geographical magazine, New York, M.

Good roads, New York, M.

Harper's monthly, New York, M.

Harper's young people, New York, W.

Harvard graduate's magazine, Boston, M.

Insect life, Washington, M. (Gift.)

International journal of ethics, Philadelphia, Q.

Johns Hopkins University Studies in historical and political science,
        Baltimore, M.

Journal of american folk-lore, Boston, Q.

Journal of comparative medicine, New York, M.

Journal of morphology, Boston, Irr.

Journal of the Franklin institute, Philadelphia, M.

Journal of zoöphily, Philadelphia, M. (Gift.)

Keynote, New York, M.

Ladies' home journal, Philadelphia, M.

Lend a hand, Boston, M.

Lippincott's magazine, Philadelphia, M.
Literary northwest, St. Paul, M.
Littell's living age, Boston, W.
Magazine of American history, New York, M.
Magazine of christian literature, New York, M.
Magazine of poetry, Buffalo, Q.
Monist, Chicago, Q.
Mother's nursery guide, New York, M.
Music, Chicago, M.
National magazine, New York, M.
New England historical and genealogical register, Boston, Q.
New England magazine, Boston, M.
New review, New York, M.
New world, Boston, Q.
North American review, New York, M.
Northwestern business educator, Milwaukee, M.   (Gift.)
Official gazette of the U. S. patent office, Washington, W.   (Gift.)
Outing, New York, M.
Overland monthly, San Francisco, M.
Pedagogical seminary, Worcester, Mass., 3 times yearly.
Philosophical review, Boston, Q.
Photographic times, New York, W.   (Gift.)
Poet lore, Boston, M.
Political science quarterly, Boston, Q.
Popular science monthly, New York, M.
Popular science news, Boston, M.
Power, New York, M.
Pratt institute monthly, Brooklyn, M.
Quarterly journal of economics, Boston, Q.
Quarterly register of current history, Detroit, Q.
Railroad and engineering journal, New York, M.
Review of reviews, New York, M.
St. Nicholas, New York, M.
Sanitarian, New York, M.
Scientific American, architects' and builders' edition, New York, M.
Scribner's magazine, New York, M.
Shakespeariana, New York, Q.
Social economist, New York, M.
Spirit of the times, New York, W.
Truth-seeker, New York, W.   (Gift.)
United service, Philadelphia, M.

University extension, Philadelphia, M.
Werner's voice magazine, New York, M.
Whist, Milwaukee, M.
Wide awake, Boston, M.
Yale review, Boston, Q.

FRANCE.

Revue de famille, Paris, SM.
Revue des deux mondes, Paris, SM.
Revue encyclopédique, Paris, SM.

GERMANY.

Deutsche revue, Berlin, M.
Deutsche rundschau, Berlin, M.
Dingler's polytechnishes journal, Stuttgart, W.
Gegenwart, Leipzig, W.
Geographische mittheilungen, Gotha, M.
Nord und süd, Breslau, M.
Unsere zeit, Leipzig, M.
Vom fels zum meer, Stuttgart, M.
Westermann's monatshefte, Brunswick, M.
Zeitschrift für vergleichende litteraturgeschichte, Berlin, Q.

GREAT BRITAIN AND IRELAND.

All the year round, London, W.
Antiquary, London, M.
Argosy, London, M.
Belgravia, London, M.
Blackwood's Edinburgh magazine, Edinburgh, M.
Chambers's journal, Edinburgh, M.
Chemical trade journal, Manchester, W.
Contemporary review, London, M.
Cornhill magazine, London, M.
Dublin review, Dublin, Q.
Edinburgh review, Edinburgh, Q.
Engineering, London, W.
English historical review, London, Q.
English illustrated magazine, London, M.
Fortnightly review, London, M.
Gentleman's magazine, London, M.
Geographical society's proceedings, London, M.

Good words, London, M.
Journal of the Anthropological institute, London, M.
Journal of the Statistical society, London, Q.
Knowledge, London, M.
London society, London, M.
Longman's magazine, London, M.
Macmillan's magazine, London, M.
Mind, London, Q.
Month, London, M.
National review, London, M.
Nature, London, W.
Nineteenth century, London, M.
Notes and queries, London, W.
Observatory, London, M.
Oil and colourman's journal, London, M.
Quarterly review, London, Q.
Review of reviews, London, M.
Scottish geographical magazine, Edinburgh, M.
Temple bar, London, M.
Westminster review, London, M.

IN THE REFERENCE ROOM.

Architectural review, Boston, 8 times yearly.
Art amateur, New York, M.
Art journal, London, M.
Illustrated world's fair, Chicago, M.
Magazine of art, London, M.
Portfolio, London, M.
World's Columbian exposition, Chicago, M.

IN THE LIBRARIAN'S ROOM.

Allgemeine bibliographie für Deutschland, Leipzig, W.
American bookmaker, M.
Appleton's literary bulletin, New York, M.   (Gift of the publishers.)
Bibliographie de la France, Paris, W.
Book buyer, New York, M.
Book chat, New York, M.
Book reviews, New York, M.   (Gift.)
Book worm, London, M.
Catalogue mensuel de la librairie française, Paris, M.

Centralblatt für bibliothekswesen, Leipzig, M.
Deutsche litteraturzeitung, Berlin, W.
Hinrichs' Bücherverzeichniss, Leipzig, Q and SA.
Johns Hopkins university circulars, Baltimore, M. (Gift of the pubs.)
Library, London, M. .
Library journal, New York, M.
Literary light, Minneapolis, M.
Literary news, New York, M.
Literary world, Boston, SM.
Litterarischer merkur, Leipzig, SM.
Notes on new books, New York, Q. (Gift.)
Publishers' circular, London, SM.
Publishers' weekly, N. Y., W.
U. S. government publications monthly catalogue, Wash., M.

Explanation of abbreviations used to denote frequency of publication: SD—twice a day; D—daily; W—weekly; SW—twice a week; BW—every two weeks; SM—twice a month; M—monthly; BM—every two months; Q—four times a year; SA—twice a year.

CONTENTS.

CPSIA information can be obtained
at www.ICGtesting.com
Printed in the USA
BVHW04*0633190718
521944BV00031B/215/P